LA CONFIRMACIÓN
para adolescentes

CONFIRMATION
for teens

FOOD FOR OUR GREAT JOURNEY

Life has often been compared to a journey, an adventure toward wholeness and happiness, toward peace and fulfillment. Many of our most difficult moments are those in which we must decide which "path" to take. Especially during our adolescent years, the road that leads us to genuine happiness and inner peace is often very difficult to see.

ALIMENTO PARA EL GRAN VIAJE DE LA VIDA

Se compara comúnmente a la vida con un viaje, con una aventura hacia la plenitud y la felicidad, hacia la paz y la realización. Algunos de los momentos más difíciles de nuestra vida son aquellos en los que no sabemos qué camino tomar; en particular durante nuestros años de adolescencia, el camino que nos lleva a la verdadera felicidad y a la paz interior no es nada fácil de encontrar.

LESSON 1 DEBBIE REPP LECCIÓN 1

JESUS SAID, "FOR WHERE TWO OR THREE ARE GATHERED IN MY NAME, I AM THERE AMONG THEM."

MATTHEW 18:20

Our society suggests a variety of appealing options. Movies, magazines, the media, and sometimes even our parents and educators make the "economic pathway to happiness" look like a sure thing. On this road, a high-paying job, financial security, and lots of material possessions become very important.

The "pathway of power and fame" appears even more glamorous—how often our heroes are outstanding athletes or beautiful movie stars. (And aren't these people always happy?) The world in which we live lures us toward these roads—and toward many more with grand appearances. We are bombarded with messages that tell us that wealth, fame, power, and physical attractiveness are all directly linked to contentment in one's life.

For the true Christian, however, there is more. Much more. The mature Christian knows that money, power, and fame have little—if anything—to do with genuine happiness. These things, in fact, too often leave us empty and aching.

The mature Christian knows that life is indeed a journey—a journey of faith! It is a journey that lasts a lifetime. The Christian looks to Jesus for direction and strength. He or she looks to Jesus when attempting to discover "the right path."

But how do we begin to know Jesus? How do we begin to allow him to show us the way? How do we make him our food for this great journey?

ENCOUNTERS WITH CHRIST THROUGH OUR CHURCH

The Catholic Church offers help in our quest to know and be strengthened by Jesus. First, it offers a community of believers. We will not be alone in our Christian lives. Others will be with us. These others—the people of God—will be a major source of strength as we journey.

Jesus said, "For where two or three are gathered in my name, I am there among them" (Matthew 18:20). In the gathering of the community, the presence of Christ is found. Without the community, we could not follow the road Jesus calls us to travel. His word comes to us through this community. We become sons and daughters of God and heirs to heaven through baptism into this community. We are nourished in this community with the Eucharist, the body of Christ broken and shared by these people.

The Catholic Church also offers us the sacramental life as a way to encounter Christ. Traditionally, a sacrament has been defined as "an outward sign, instituted by Christ, to give grace." Put more simply, a sacrament is a special moment in our Catholic life in which outward signs and rituals bring us into a very intense closeness to Jesus. Through human ministries, Jesus is actually forgiving us, nourishing

Nuestra sociedad sugiere una gran variedad de opciones atractivas: películas, revistas, medios de comunicación. En ocasiones, nuestros padres o educadores ven en lo económico el camino seguro hacia la felicidad. En este camino, lo importante es contar con un sueldo alto, con seguridad financiera y poseer muchas cosas.

Los caminos del poder y de la fama se muestran más atractivos aún. ¿Cuántas veces nuestros héroes son grandes atletas o bellas estrellas de cine? Y, ¿acaso esta gente no es siempre feliz? El mundo en el que vivimos nos orienta hacia estos caminos y a muchos otros que son mera apariencia. Nos bombardean con mensajes que proclaman que la riqueza, la fama, el poder y la belleza física van de la mano con la felicidad en nuestra vida.

No obstante, para el verdadero cristiano hay algo más, mucho más. El cristiano maduro sabe que el dinero, el poder y la fama tienen poco que ver, si no es que nada que ver, con la felicidad auténtica. De hecho, estas cosas nos dejan normalmente vacíos y afligidos. El cristiano maduro sabe que la vida es en realidad un viaje, un viaje de fe. Se trata de un viaje que se prolonga durante toda la vida. El cristiano mira a Jesús para encontrar orientación y fortaleza. Él o ella, cuando intentan encontrar "el camino correcto", miran a Jesús.

¿Cómo comenzamos a conocer a Jesús? ¿Cómo permitirle que nos muestre el camino? ¿Cómo hacemos de Él nuestro alimento para nuestro gran viaje?

ENCUENTROS CON CRISTO A TRAVÉS DE NUESTRA IGLESIA

La Iglesia Católica nos brinda su ayuda en la búsqueda por conocer y fortalecernos en Jesús. En primer lugar, ofrece una comunidad de creyentes. No estamos solos en nuestra vida cristiana. Otros están a nuestro lado. Estos otros, el pueblo de Dios, será la mayor fuente de fortaleza para este viaje.

Jesús dijo: "donde están dos o tres reunidos en mi Nombre, allí estoy yo, en medio de ellos" (Mt 18:20). En la reunión de la comunidad se encuentra la presencia de Cristo. Sin la comunidad no podríamos seguir el camino que Jesús nos llama a recorrer. Su palabra llega a nosotros por medio de esta comunidad. A través del Bautismo dentro de esta comunidad, nos convertimos en hijos e hijas de Dios y en herederos, además, del Cielo. En esta comunidad, se nos nutre con la Eucaristía, Cuerpo de Cristo fragmentado y repartido entre nosotros.

JESÚS DIJO: "DONDE ESTÁN DOS O TRES REUNIDOS EN MI NOMBRE, ALLÍ ESTOY YO, EN MEDIO DE ELLOS" (MT 18:20).

QUESTIONS TO CONSIDER

- What does it mean to be "a child of God?"
- What meaning does your baptism have for you today?
- The oil (chrism) of our baptism reminds us that we are "Priest, Prophet, and King" (from the *Order of Baptism of Children*). Yet, our society defines our values in many destructive ways. Can you give an example of how our modern world defines our values?

(Recall the "roads to success" discussed earlier in this lesson.)

us, healing us. We are, in these very personal encounters with Christ, receiving his power so that we can follow in his footsteps.

Through the sacraments, we receive grace—a gift from God. We do not "earn" grace through our commitments or studies. Grace is always freely given by our generous Lord who wishes to empower us through his marvelous and mysterious influence.
The sacraments require faith because they involve "mystery."

In the weeks ahead, you will be more fully introduced to the richness of the sacrament of confirmation—
a sacrament intimately linked to our baptism. Confirmation, like all sacraments, begins with a ritual, but the graces received are experienced in every moment of our great journey.

QUESTIONS TO CONSIDER

When we were baptized, it is likely we were too young to remember this wonderful sacrament in which we were welcomed and embraced by the Christian community. We became children of God. One of the objectives of adolescent confirmation is to give young men and women a sense of their own dignity and value because of their baptisms…because they are God's precious children. Recalling our baptisms helps us to reflect on our great value at a time when we might be doubting it.

La Confirmación para adolescentes

Confirmation for teens

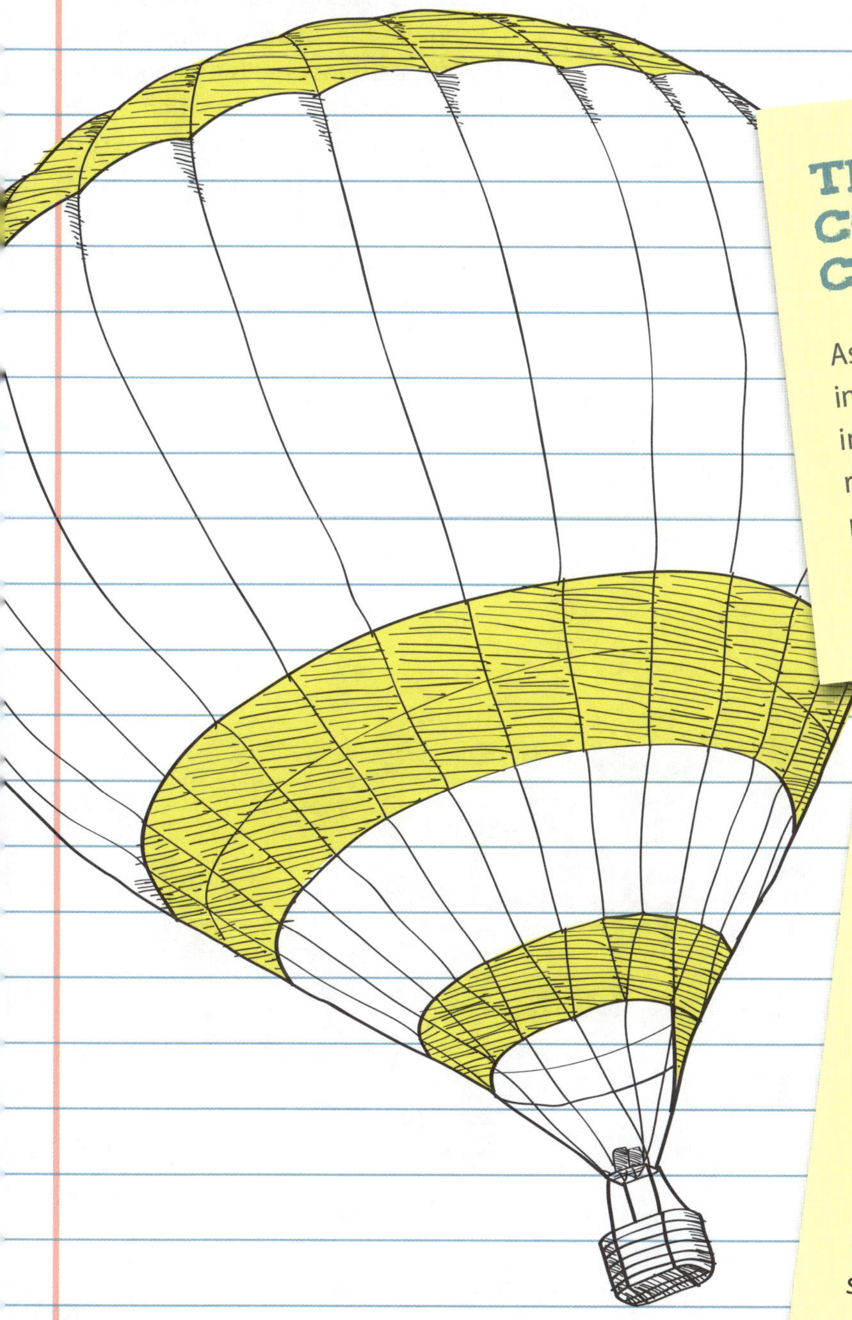

THE PARISH COMMITMENT CEREMONY

As you prepare to receive the gifts of the Holy Spirit in the sacrament of confirmation, you will become involved in a period of important study, prayer, reflection, and service. It is most valuable if your parish family is fully aware of your efforts so that it can support you through prayer.

LA CEREMONIA DE COMPROMISO EN LA PARROQUIA

Al prepararte para recibir los dones del Espíritu Santo por medio del sacramento de la Confirmación, estarás participando en un periodo muy importante de estudio, oración, reflexión y servicio. Es importante que la familia parroquial sea consciente de tu trabajo, para que te pueda sostener con sus oraciones.

LESSON 2 | DEBBIE REPP | LECCIÓN 2

In **Lesson One**, we discussed how the Catholic Church offers us a community of believers so that we are never alone as we journey toward Christian maturity. Jesus tells us, "For where two or three are gathered in my name, I am there among them" (Matthew 18:20). In the gathering of the community, the very real presence of Christ is found. Without the community, it would become most difficult, if not impossible, to follow Christ. His word comes to us **through this community**. We became sons and daughters of God and heirs to heaven through baptism into this community. We are nourished in this community with the Eucharist, the body of Christ broken and shared by these people.

In confirmation, too, the community is essential. It is the faith community in which you worship that calls you to become stronger members. And **you have much to give** to the community! Your church needs the deeper faith, courage, and energy that new members can bring. In return, it responds to your desire for confirmation through its welcoming and its prayers. Though you are young, you are fully recognized as people of faith entering a very important time of preparation and discernment. Therefore, your parish family offers you its reassurance and support.

The prayer service which follows will ideally occur following the homily during a Sunday eucharistic celebration. The "Parish Commitment Ceremony" gives you the opportunity to promise to do your best to understand the sacrament of confirmation. (It is not your commitment to receive the sacrament—that comes much later!)

The ceremony also informs the parish family of **your intentions** so that all its members can be spiritually present with you as you journey.

Note: Parishes vary widely on when they ask confirmation candidates to select their "sponsors." If you have chosen a sponsor, ask him or her to be present with you at the "Parish Commitment Ceremony," but your sponsor's presence is not essential at this time. If no sponsors are present at the ceremony, omit the section of the ceremony entitled "To the Confirmation Sponsors."

This short service can fit into a paraliturgy or the eucharistic liturgy. It should be preceded by a reading from Scripture and followed by prayers for God's blessings on this preparation for the sacrament of confirmation. A homily by the priest or deacon or an encouragement from the catechist would also be appropriate before the "commitment to prepare." The celebrant names, one at a time, the candidates for confirmation. As the names are called, **each will stand** with his or her sponsor. The Words of Commitment follow.

"IN THE GATHERING OF THE COMMUNITY, THE VERY REAL PRESENCE OF CHRIST IS FOUND."

"CUANDO LA COMUNIDAD SE REÚNE, CRISTO SE ENCUENTRA REALMENTE PRESENTE"

En la **lección uno** comentamos cómo la Iglesia Católica pone a nuestra disposición una comunidad de creyentes, de modo que nunca estemos solos en nuestro camino hacia la madurez cristiana. Jesús nos dice: "Pues donde están dos o tres reunidos en mi nombre, allí estoy yo, en medio de ellos" (Mt 18:20). En la reunión de la comunidad, se encuentra la verdadera presencia de Cristo. Sin la comunidad sería más difícil, quizás imposible, seguir a Cristo. Su palabra llega a nosotros **por medio de la comunidad**. Nosotros llegamos a ser hijos e hijas de Dios y herederos del Cielo por medio del Bautismo dentro de esta comunidad. Somos alimentados en esta comunidad con la Eucaristía, con el cuerpo de Cristo fragmentado y distribuido en esta comunidad.

De la misma manera, la comunidad es esencial en la Confirmación. Es la comunidad de fe en la que tú das culto, la que te anima a ser un mejor miembro. Y **tú tienes mucho que dar** a la comunidad. Tu parroquia necesita de una fe más profunda, del coraje y la energía que nuevos miembros puedan traer. A cambio de eso, ella responde a tu deseo de confirmarte, te da la bienvenida y te apoya con sus oraciones. Aunque estás joven, se te reconoce como una persona de fe que inicia un periodo importante de preparación y discernimiento. Por lo tanto, tu familia parroquial te ofrece su alivio y apoyo.

La oración que se presenta a continuación, podría decirse después de la homilía durante la Celebración Eucarística del domingo. La Ceremonia de Compromiso de la Parroquia te da la oportunidad de prometer que harás tu mejor esfuerzo para comprender lo que es el sacramento de la Confirmación (no se trata aún del compromiso para recibir el sacramento, ese compromiso se hará después).

En la ceremonia también se informa a la comunidad parroquial **acerca de tus intenciones**, de modo que todos sus miembros puedan acompañarte espiritualmente en tu camino.

Nota: Las parroquias difieren mucho acerca del momento en que los candidatos a la Confirmación eligen a sus padrinos. Si ya has elegido a tu padrino, pídele que esté presente contigo durante la "Ceremonia de Compromiso de la Parroquia". Sin embargo, la presencia de los padrinos no es esencial para esta ceremonia. Si no hay padrinos presentes en la ceremonia, se puede omitir la parte titulada: "A los padrinos de Confirmación".

Esta breve ceremonia puede realizarse también en una paraliturgia o durante la Liturgia Eucarística. Debe estar precedida de una lectura de la Escritura y seguida de las oraciones para recibir las bendiciones de Dios durante esta preparación para el sacramento de la Confirmación. Sería apropiado que el sacerdote o el diácono ofreciera una homilía; incluso podrían llegar a ser muy adecuadas algunas palabras de aliento por parte de un catequista. A medida que se van anunciando sus nombres, **cada uno se pondrá de pie** junto con su padrino. Las palabras de compromiso se pronuncian enseguida.

THE WORDS OF COMMITMENT

TO THE CONFIRMATION CANDIDATES

Celebrant: God has called you to be God's sons and daughters in the sacrament of baptism. You have followed the Light. Now the way of the gospel opens more fully before you, inviting you to acknowledge God's love for you by asking you to commit yourself to a life of service and love, peace and justice to all. This is the way of faith on which Christ will lovingly guide you to eternal life. Are you ready to enter this journey?

Candidates: I am.

Celebrant: Are you willing to accept the Christian community as your environment for experiencing faith and growing in the Spirit?

Candidates: I am.

Celebrant: Are you willing to deepen your personal commitment to Jesus Christ and take responsibility for the gifts of the Spirit in order to help build the kingdom of God?

Candidates: I am.

TO THE CONFIRMATION SPONSORS

Celebrant: Are you willing to help guide these candidates for confirmation in the name of this Christian community on their journey of the Spirit?

Sponsors: I am.

TO THE PARISH COMMUNITY

Celebrant: Will you continue to renew your faith in the spirit of your own confirmation?

Community: Yes, we will.

Celebrant: Will you also support these young men and women of our Christian community as they follow Jesus and his gospel?

Community: Yes, we will.

Celebrant: Lord of love and mercy, we thank you in the name of our brothers and sisters, who have experienced your guiding presence in their lives. Today, in the presence of your community, they are promising to prepare for your coming in the sacrament of confirmation. *(The celebrant now asks the sponsors to sign the candidates to prepare them for the journey of the Spirit.)*

Receive the cross of Christ: By this sign of his love, Christ will be your strength. Learn now to know and follow him. Remember that he is your faithful companion as you study, reflect, prepare, and pray.

Candidates: Amen

Celebrant: Lord, we pray for those just signed with the cross of our Lord Jesus Christ. By its power, keep them safe. May they be faithful to the call so that they can live with their beloved Creator in glory. We ask this through Christ our Lord.

All: Amen

Prayer of the Faithful follows.

La Confirmación para adolescentes

Confirmation for teens

Baptism Confirmation Eucharist

Our introduction to the life of the Church

In the Catholic tradition, baptism, confirmation, and Eucharist are known as the sacraments of initiation. Initiation is formally defined as "the rites, ceremonies, etc. observed in admitting a candidate into a society or organization." It includes "instruction in the first principles" of the society or organization. Through these "initiation rites," new members experience a definite acceptance into the society and are expected to participate more fully in the activities and life of the society.

Bautismo, Confirmación y Eucaristía

Nuestra introducción a la vida de la Iglesia

En la tradición católica, el Bautismo, la Confirmación y la Eucaristía, son conocidos como los sacramentos de iniciación. La iniciación se define formalmente como los ritos, las ceremonias, etc., que se observan para admitir a un candidato dentro de una sociedad u organización. Esto implica la instrucción en los principios primarios de la sociedad u organización. Por medio de estos ritos de iniciación, los nuevos miembros viven la experiencia de ser aceptados dentro de la sociedad, quien espera de ellos que participen más de lleno en sus actividades y, en general, en la vida de la sociedad.

LESSON 3

DEBBIE REPP

LECCIÓN 3

Baptism, confirmation, and Eucharist—as sacraments of initiation—are our introduction to the life of the Catholic Church. Even though in our present experience these three sacraments take place over a long period of time, **initially, they were celebrated at one time**. After a long period of instruction centered on the beliefs of the Creed, the candidates (called catechumens) presented themselves to the Christian community for acceptance.

In the way that new members of the Catholic faith are presently welcomed into the Church on Holy Saturday night, candidates were baptized. On that same evening, the candidates were confirmed, signifying their personal faith commitment to be active members of their new Christian community. Then, **for the first time**, the new Christians were able to participate in the entire eucharistic liturgy and receive holy Communion. Since all three sacraments—baptism, confirmation, and Eucharist—were given at one time to new members of the Church, they were known as the sacraments of initiation.

This is still the order in which new adult Catholics receive the sacraments **on Holy Saturday night**. In a later lesson, we will discuss how these three sacraments came to be separated. There remains much discussion and debate within the Church as to when and at what age it is most appropriate to receive the sacrament of confirmation. Most catechists (those who instruct us in the beliefs of our faith), however, continue to regard confirmation as a "sacrament of initiation."

WE ARE CLAIMED FOR CHRIST BY OUR BAPTISM

When we were younger, perhaps even shortly after our birth, our parents started the "initiation process" for us by asking God's Church to baptize us. We were brought into the faith of the Church. The priest said to our parents: "You have asked to have your child baptized. In doing so, you have accepted the responsibility of training your child in the faith. It will be your duty to bring your child up to keep God's commandments as Christ taught you, by loving God and your neighbor." The ceremony continued with even more dramatic emphasis on the Christian community welcoming us into its life. "My dear child, the **Christian community welcomes you** with great joy. In its name, I claim you for Christ, our Savior, by the sign of this cross."

Baptism not only focused on our beginning journey into the faith of the community but also strongly stressed that we were loved by God and became God's very own. The Father of Jesus Christ became our Father, too. We are unconditionally accepted and loved by God. As we learned in Lesson One, our baptism gives us great intrinsic value. If for no other reason, we must see ourselves as precious and worthy of love simply because we are children of the Lord.

MY DEAR CHILD, THE CHRISTIAN COMMUNITY WELCOMES YOU WITH GREAT JOY. IN ITS NAME, I CLAIM YOU FOR CHRIST, OUR SAVIOR, BY THE SIGN OF THIS CROSS.

El Bautismo, la Confirmación y la Eucaristía, como sacramentos de iniciación, son nuestra introducción a la vida de la Iglesia Católica. Aunque en nuestra experiencia presente estos tres sacramentos se llevan a cabo a lo largo de un periodo bastante extenso, en un inicio **se celebraban todos en una misma ceremonia**. Después de un largo periodo de instrucción acerca del Credo, los candidatos, llamados catecúmenos, se presentaban a la comunidad para ser aceptados.

Del mismo modo en que los nuevos miembros de la fe católica son recibidos actualmente en la Iglesia durante la noche del Sábado Santo, así eran bautizados los candidatos. En un inicio, esa misma noche los candidatos eran confirmados, lo cual significaba un compromiso personal de fe para ser miembros activos de su nueva comunidad cristiana. Después, **por primera vez**, los nuevos cristianos podían participar en toda la Celebración Eucarística y recibir la Santa Comunión. Dado que los tres sacramentos, Bautismo, Confirmación y Eucaristía, se impartían a un mismo tiempo a los nuevos miembros de la Iglesia, estos eran conocidos como los sacramentos de iniciación.

Este es el mismo orden en el que los nuevos católicos adultos reciben los sacramentos **durante la noche del Sábado Santo**. En una lección posterior se discutirá el modo en que estos tres sacramentos pueden dividirse. Actualmente hay algo de discusión y debate dentro de la Iglesia sobre cuándo y a qué edad es más apropiada la recepción del sacramento de la Confirmación. Sin embargo, la mayoría de los catequistas (aquellos que nos introducen en las creencias de nuestra fe), siguen refiriéndose a la Confirmación como un "un sacramento de iniciación".

CRISTO NOS RECUPERA A TRAVÉS DE NUESTRO BAUTISMO

Cuando éramos muy pequeños, quizá poco después de nacer, nuestros padres dieron inicio a nuestro proceso de iniciación, pidiendo a la Iglesia de Dios que nos bautizara. Fuimos introducidos en la fe de la Iglesia. El sacerdote dijo a nuestros padres: "Ustedes han pedido que su niño sea bautizado. Al hacer esta petición, han aceptado la responsabilidad de educar a su hijo en la fe. Será deber suyo educar a su hijo en el respeto por los mandamientos de Dios, así como Cristo los enseñó, "amando a Dios y al prójimo". La ceremonia continúa enfatizando la bienvenida que la comunidad cristiana nos da dentro de su vida. "Querido hijo, **la comunidad cristiana te da la bienvenida** con gran alegría. En su nombre, te reclamo para Cristo salvador nuestro, por medio del signo de la cruz".

El Bautismo no solo se centra en el inicio de nuestro viaje en la fe de una comunidad, sino también recalca enérgicamente que somos amados por Dios y que nos ha hecho de su propiedad. El Padre de Jesucristo se convirtió también en Padre de

QUERIDO HIJO, LA COMUNIDAD CRISTIANA TE DA LA BIENVENIDA CON GRAN ALEGRÍA. EN SU NOMBRE, TE RECLAMO PARA CRISTO SALVADOR NUESTRO, POR MEDIO DEL SIGNO DE LA CRUZ.

QUESTIONS TO CONSIDER

Your preparation for the sacrament of confirmation should include some real soul-searching. It is important to ask yourself the questions, "What does my baptism mean to me? What does it mean to have life in the Church?"

To help you answer these difficult questions, pretend, for a moment, that you were never baptized. Imagine that your parents and godparents never initiated you into the Christian community. Describe, in as much detail as possible, how your life would be different. (For example, what kind of moral framework might you have if you never knew Jesus? Would you have different friends? Perhaps a different school? How would you celebrate special days like Christmas and Easter if Jesus was not part of your life? Would you view death differently?) Hopefully, by imagining your life without the special sacraments of initiation, you might better be able to recognize and appreciate the many ways in which God's gift of grace influences and affects your life.

IN CONFIRMATION, EMPOWERED BY THE SPIRIT, WE MAKE THE FAITH OUR OWN

Baptism brings a person into the faith of the Church. As a small baby or child, we are completely passive, but the grace of God is freely given to us. Confirmation, as it is now celebrated, is largely the "active" part of the initiation process. The baptized Christian takes the faith that was given and makes it his or her own. A candidate for confirmation, after careful review of what the Church teaches, seeks to accept these teachings as his or her own. And with acceptance must come deliberate and active involvement in the life of the faith community.

IN THE EUCHARIST, OUR SPIRITS ARE NOURISHED

Another name for Jesus' death and Resurrection is the "paschal mystery." Jesus is our "Lamb of God." He allowed himself to be killed, and through his suffering and death on the cross, we are able to live. In the Eucharist, this paschal mystery is celebrated. In response to Christ's gift of himself to us, we bring to God our own lives—symbolized in the bread and wine, "the work of human hands." God accepts our lives, consecrates them, and nourishes our spirits through his special presence in the Eucharist.

La Confirmación para adolescentes

Confirmation for teens

WE BELIEVE

In the previous lessons, you learned that confirmation is one of the sacraments of initiation. Usually, before choosing to become fully initiated into a group or organization, it is wise to have a firm understanding of the beliefs, goals, and purposes of the group or organization. As a simple example, if you have an interest in becoming a writer for your high school newspaper, you would likely study the newspaper to see if it contains articles you would enjoy researching and writing.

CREEMOS

En las lecciones anteriores aprendiste que la Confirmación es uno de los sacramentos de iniciación. Normalmente, antes de elegir formar parte de algún grupo u organización, es necesario tener una clara idea de las creencias, las metas y propósitos de ese grupo u organización. Como ejemplo claro, si tienes interés por escribir para el periódico de tu escuela, es muy probable que hagas una búsqueda en el periódico para ver si hay algún artículo sobre el que te gustaría investigar o escribir. También te gustaría ver cuándo se realiza alguna junta de la editorial, de cuánto tiempo dispone un escritor para redactar un artículo y cosas por el estilo. Una vez que ya entiendes bien el funcionamiento y los requisitos de un periódico, serás capaz de tomar una decisión bien informada para aceptar o rechazar el trabajo como redactor del periódico.

LESSON 4 | DEBBIE REPP | LECCIÓN 4

You might also find out when editorial meetings take place, what kind of time commitment a staff writer needs to make, and so on. Once you have a good understanding of the newspaper's function and requirements, you will be able to make a well-informed decision about whether or not to join the staff of writers.

With the help of the Holy Spirit, confirmation involves your commitment to become fully immersed in the life of the Church. Remember, confirmation is the active part of the initiation process. Therefore, preparation for confirmation requires careful and thoughtful study of the teachings of the Catholic Church. The better you understand the Church and its teachings, the more mature your decision to become an active and committed member.

In this lesson, we will review some of the most important beliefs of the Catholic community as revealed in our belief statements (the Nicene Creed and the Apostles' Creed) and in guidelines set forth by sacred Scripture (the Ten Commandments and the Beatitudes). Study these teachings carefully. **Make sure you understand the meaning of each statement. Do not hesitate to ask for clarification if something does not make sense to you. When you ask questions, you open the door to greater understanding and growth.**

THE NICENE CREED

In the year 325, the Church leaders met in the town of Nicaea to consider what the Church held as sacred doctrine. This Council, drawing upon three hundred years of lived faith, formulated a creed that we still say every Sunday at Mass. Containing 14 different belief statements, it summarized many of the most important teachings of the community.

I believe in one God,
the Father almighty,
maker of heaven and earth,
of all things visible and invisible.

I believe in one Lord Jesus Christ,
the Only Begotten Son of God,
born of the Father before all ages.
God from God, Light from Light,
true God from true God,
begotten, not made,
consubstantial with the Father;
through him all things were made.
For us men and for our salvation
he came down from heaven,
and by the Holy Spirit
was incarnate of the Virgin Mary, and became man.
For our sake he was crucified under Pontius Pilate,
he suffered death and was buried,
and rose again on the third day
in accordance with the Scriptures.
He ascended into heaven
and is seated at the right hand of the Father.
He will come again in glory
to judge the living and the dead
and his kingdom will have no end.

I believe in the Holy Spirit,
the Lord, the giver of life,
who proceeds from the Father and the Son,
who with the Father and the Son
is adored and glorified,
who has spoken through the prophets.

I believe in one, holy, catholic and apostolic Church.
I confess one Baptism
for the forgiveness of sins
and I look forward to the resurrection of the dead
and the life of the world to come.
Amen.

La Confirmación implica un compromiso de participar en la vida de la Iglesia. Para eso cuentas con la ayuda del Espíritu Santo. Recuerda que la Confirmación es la parte activa de este proceso de iniciación. Por lo tanto, la preparación para la Confirmación requiere un cuidadoso y atento estudio de las enseñanzas de la Iglesia Católica. Mientras mejor entiendas a la Iglesia y sus enseñanzas, tu decisión de convertirte en un miembro activo y comprometido de ella será más madura.

En esta lección repasaremos algunas de las creencias más importantes de la comunidad católica, tal como se muestran en nuestras declaraciones de fe (el Credo de Nicea y el Credo de los Apóstoles) y en las directrices establecidas por la Sagrada Escritura (los Diez Mandamientos y las Bienaventuranzas). Estudia cuidadosamente estas enseñanzas. **Asegúrate de entender el significado de cada declaración. No dudes en pedir alguna explicación si hay algo que no tenga sentido para ti. Al hacer preguntas, abres la puerta para alcanzar una mejor comprensión y crecimiento.**

EL CREDO DE NICEA

En el año 325, los líderes de la Iglesia se reunieron en la ciudad de Nicea, para considerar lo que la Iglesia sostenía como Doctrina Sagrada. Este Concilio, basado en 300 años de fe vivida, formuló un credo que aún recitamos en cada Misa dominical. Contiene catorce diferentes formulaciones de fe y resume la mayoría de las enseñanzas más importantes de la comunidad.

Creo en un solo Dios,
Padre Todopoderoso,
Creador del cielo y de la tierra,
de todo lo visible y lo invisible.

Creo en un solo Señor, Jesucristo,
Hijo único de Dios,
nacido del Padre antes de todos los siglos: Dios de Dios, Luz de Luz,
Dios verdadero de Dios verdadero,
engendrado, no creado,
de la misma naturaleza del Padre,
por quien todo fue hecho;
que por nosotros, los hombres, y por nuestra salvación bajó del cielo,
y por obra del Espíritu Santo se encarnó de María, la Virgen, y se hizo hombre;
y por nuestra causa fue crucificado en tiempos de Poncio Pilato;
padeció
y fue sepultado,
y resucitó al tercer día, según las Escrituras,
y subió al Cielo,
y está sentado a la derecha del Padre;
y de nuevo vendrá con gloria para juzgar a vivos y muertos,
y su reino no tendrá fin.

Creo en el Espíritu Santo,
Señor y dador de vida,
que procede del Padre y del Hijo,
que con el Padre y el Hijo recibe
una misma adoración y gloria,
y que habló por los profetas.

Creo en la Iglesia, que es una,
santa, católica y apostólica.
Confieso que hay un solo Bautismo
para el perdón de los pecados.
Espero la resurrección de los muertos
y la vida del mundo futuro.
Amén.

THE APOSTLES' CREED

The Apostles' Creed, the first prayer of the rosary, is another belief statement of the Church.

I believe in God, the Father almighty,
Creator of heaven and earth,
and in Jesus Christ, his only Son,
our Lord,
who was conceived by the Holy Spirit,
born of the Virgin Mary,
suffered under Pontius Pilate,
was crucified, died and was buried;
he descended into hell;
On the third day he rose again from
the dead;

he ascended into heaven,
and is seated at the right hand
of God the Father almighty;
from there he will come to judge
the living and the dead.

I believe in the Holy Spirit,
the holy catholic Church,
the communion of saints,
the forgiveness of sins,
the resurrection of the body,
and life everlasting. Amen.

THE TEN COMMANDMENTS

Besides the two creedal statements, which are the basic doctrinal statements of the Catholic community, two scripturally based guidelines have been standards for the moral life of Christians. The first of these Scripture passages is found in Exodus 20:1-17:

ONE I am the Lord your God, who brought you out of the land of Egypt, out of the house of slavery; you shall have no other gods before me. You shall not make for yourself an idol, whether in the form of anything that is in heaven above, or that is on the earth beneath, or that is in the waters under the earth. You shall not bow down to them or worship them; for I the Lord your God am a jealous God, punishing children for the iniquity of parents, to the third and the fourth generation of those who reject me, but showing steadfast love to the thousandth generation of those who love me and keep my commandments.

TWO You shall not make wrongful use of the name of the Lord your God, for the Lord will not acquit anyone who misuses his name.

THREE Remember the sabbath day, and keep it holy. Six days you shall labor and do all your work. But the seventh day is a sabbath to the Lord your God; you shall not do any work—you, your son or your daughter, your male or female slave, your livestock, or the alien resident in your towns. For in six days the Lord made heaven and earth, the sea, and all that is in them, but rested the seventh day; therefore the Lord blessed the sabbath day and consecrated it.

FOUR Honor your father and your mother, so that your days may be long in the land that the Lord your God is giving you.

FIVE You shall not murder.

SIX You shall not commit adultery.

SEVEN You shall not steal.

EIGHT You shall not bear false witness against your neighbor.

NINE You shall not covet your neighbor's house.

TEN You shall not covet your neighbor's wife, or male or female slave, or ox, or donkey, or anything that belongs to your neighbor.

LA CONFIRMACIÓN para adolescentes

CONFIRMATION for teens

A BRIEF HISTORY OF THE SACRAMENT

During the ceremony of confirmation, the bishop, while making the sign of the cross on your forehead with the oil of chrism, will say: **"Be sealed with the Gifts of the Holy Spirit."** You will already have stated that you believe that Jesus died and rose and ascended to the Father and sent the Spirit to empower all believers. You will have made the decision, to the best of your abilities, to take an active part in the life of the Church. With the help of the Holy Spirit, you will commit yourself to the great task of spreading the Gospel of Jesus through your loving actions and words. Confirmation day will be a celebration of your conversion to a full and active sharing in the work of the Lord.

UNA BREVE HISTORIA DEL SACRAMENTO

Durante la ceremonia de Confirmación, el obispo, al momento de hacer con el santo crisma la señal de la cruz sobre tu frente, pronunciará las siguientes palabras: **"Recibe por esta señal el Don del Espíritu Santo".** Para este momento, tú ya habrás manifestado tu fe en la muerte y resurrección de Jesús, en su ascensión al Padre y en el envío del Espíritu Santo, a fin de fortalecer a todos los creyentes. Habrás tomado también la decisión de ser un miembro activo dentro de la vida de la Iglesia, en la medida de tus posibilidades. Con la ayuda del Espíritu Santo te comprometerás a realizar la gran tarea de predicar el Evangelio de Jesús, por medio de tu palabra y por medio de tus acciones, hechas con amor. El día de la Confirmación será una celebración de la transformación de tu vida, transformación que conlleva entrega activa y total a la obra del Señor.

In this belief, **you are in union with fellow Christians through the centuries**. Read, for instance, the words of Saint Cyril of Jerusalem, a bishop from the fourth century. His words still speak to each of us:

> *To you who are soon to be enlightened.... Already you have gathered round the vestibule of the King's palace; may you also be led into the banquet hall by the King!...*
>
> *Please be aware of how great a dignity Jesus bestows on you.... The indwelling Spirit makes your mind a house of God. Once you have heard what is written concerning the mysteries, then will you understand things which you cannot grasp now....*
>
> *Let me give you this charge also. Study our teachings and keep them forever....Let your mind be refined as by fire unto reverence; let your soul be forged as metal. Let the stubbornness of unbelief be hammered out....Let the gate of Paradise be opened to every man and every woman among you....May he fill you with the heavenly things of the new covenant and give you the seal of the Holy Spirit in Christ Jesus our Lord.*
>
> *To him be the glory forever and ever! Amen*

(From the Prologue of the Catechetical Lectures entitled, "Address of Saint Cyril of Jerusalem to His Catechumens").

You are being asked to study and prepare for the sacrament of confirmation during your adolescent or young adult years, but before we go further, let's look at the history of this sacrament. The celebration of this sacrament has undergone many changes, especially in the recent century.

LET YOUR MIND BE REFINED AS BY FIRE UNTO REVERENCE; LET YOUR SOUL BE FORGED AS METAL.

THE HISTORY OF CONFIRMATION

THE EARLY CHURCH AND THE CATECHUMENATE.

As the Church began to grow in the late half of the first century and into the second century, Christianity spread throughout the Near East and as far as Rome. As more Gentiles (non-Jews) began to seek membership in the Church, **a longer period of preparation** became necessary. This preparation time was called the catechumenate.

During these apostolic times, adults were initiated into the community.

At times, however, whole households (adults and children) were accepted at one time into the faith community. The children would grow up in a community and family filled with faith, and the family would be the natural setting in which faith could be experienced and nurtured.

As time progressed, the catechumenate developed more completely. The candidates participated with the Christian community in many of the meetings and celebrations before baptism. They went to Mass, for example, for the Liturgy of the Word, but were ushered out at the time of the offering of bread and wine. By the fourth century, the Church developed a complex series of rituals for this initiation process.

First of all, believing Christians (called sponsors) presented the candidates for acceptance in the catechumenate. Then an instruction period, often several years in length, followed. **The candidates were gradually introduced** to the way of living that the believing Christians shared. This lifestyle was marked with a sense

PERMITAN QUE SUS MENTES SEAN PURIFICADAS POR EL FUEGO; PERMITAN QUE SU ALMA SEA FORJADA COMO EL METAL.

Cuando vives tu fe, te pones en comunión con los demás cristianos **de todos los tiempos**. Lee, por ejemplo, las palabras de san Cirilo de Jerusalén, obispo del siglo IV. Estas palabras son válidas aún hoy:

> *A ustedes que están por ser iluminados… Ustedes ya se han reunido alrededor del vestíbulo del palacio del Rey; que ustedes sean también conducidos por el Rey a la sala del banquete… Por favor, sean conscientes de la gran dignidad que Cristo les confiere… El Espíritu, que mora en ustedes, hace de sus mentes la casa de Dios. Una vez que hayan escuchado lo que está escrito acerca de los misterios, serán capaces de entender cosas que aún no pueden comprender en su totalidad… Permítanme que les dé también esta tarea: estudien nuestras enseñanzas y guárdenlas para siempre… Permitan que sus mentes sean purificadas por el fuego; permitan que su alma sea forjada como el metal. Dejen que la terquedad para creer sea eliminada… Permitan que la puerta del Paraíso se abra para cada hombre y mujer que esté entre ustedes… Que Él los llene de las cosas celestiales de la Nueva Alianza y los marque con el sello del Espíritu Santo en Cristo Jesús, Nuestro Señor. A Él la gloria por los siglos de los siglos. Amén.*

(Del prólogo de los sermones catequéticos titulado, "Discurso de san Cirilo de Jerusalén a los catecúmenos").

A ustedes se les pide que estudien y se preparen durante su adolescencia o edad joven para el sacramento de la Confirmación. Pero antes de seguir adelante, echemos una mirada a la historia del sacramento. La celebración de este sacramento ha sufrido muchos cambios, en especial en los últimos siglos.

HISTORIA DE LA CONFIRMACIÓN

LA IGLESIA PRIMITIVA Y LOS CATECÚMENOS

A medida que la Iglesia comenzó a crecer a mediados del siglo primero e inicios del segundo, el Cristianismo fue esparciéndose desde el Oriente Próximo hasta Roma. Ante la búsqueda de más gentiles (no judíos) que querían ser miembros de la Iglesia, fue necesario **un periodo más largo de preparación**. Este tiempo de preparación fue llamado "catecumenado".

Durante el tiempo de los Apóstoles, los adultos eran iniciados en las comunidades. En ocasiones, incluso familias enteras (niños y adultos), eran aceptadas en la comunidad de fe. Los niños crecían en una comunidad y en una familia creyente. La familia era el lugar natural para que experimentaran y nutrieran su fe.

Al pasar del tiempo, el catecumenado se desarrolló cada vez más. Los candidatos participaban en varias de las reuniones y celebraciones antes de su Bautismo. Por ejemplo, participaban en la Misa hasta la liturgia de la Palabra, después de la cual, se les pedía que abandonaran la asamblea antes de ofrecer el pan y el vino. Durante el siglo IV, la Iglesia desarrolló una serie compleja de rituales para la iniciación de este proceso. Primero, los cristianos creyentes (llamados padrinos), presentaban a los candidatos para ser aceptados en el catecumenado. Seguía un periodo de instrucción que se prolongaba incluso por años. **A los candidatos se les introducía gradualmente** en el modo de vida que los creyentes compartían. Este estilo de vida

of constant conversion through the Word of God, frequent prayer, and regular periods of fasting and almsgiving. The period of being a catechumen **was a deeply spiritual time**.

The candidates who were ready for baptism were chosen, at the beginning of Lent, to prepare for the actual initiation celebration. The entire community prayed frequently for them.

Finally, at dawn on Easter morn, the candidates were led to the pool for baptism and immersed in the water, as each professed his or her faith in the Father, the Son, and the Holy Spirit. The newly baptized were then confirmed, by the bishop, with the gift of the Spirit, through the laying on of hands and anointing. The new community members completed their initiation by bringing forth the gifts of bread and wine, and sharing the Eucharist with the Christian community **for the first time**.

This intense conversion experience in the midst of the community was usually followed by another period of instruction, lasting for the 50 days of Easter, until Pentecost.

MIDDLE AGES TO MODERN TIMES

But things changed. As Christianity became the official religion of the Western world, fewer adult conversions took place. Most people belonged to the Church from infancy, when they were baptized. Confirmation came to take place just before first Communion, which **was celebrated at about the age of 12**. The bishop's presence reminded the candidates that they were members of the entire Church, not just a small-faith community. During the Middle Ages, confirmation, because it was separated from baptism, began to emphasize other characteristics of initiation. Confirmation became known as the sacrament in which one became a "soldier of Christ." The experience of confirmation itself emphasized "Christian witness" symbolized by the bishop's slight tap on the candidate's cheek.

TWENTIETH-CENTURY CHANGES

In the twentieth century, **a major change** in the initiation process occurred. Pope Pius X wanted children to experience the Eucharist earlier, so he introduced the practice of first Communion at the "age of reason," around 7 or 8. Confirmation, however, continued to be received around the age of 12 in most dioceses. This meant that the traditional order of the sacraments of initiation—baptism, confirmation, and Eucharist—had been disrupted. This change in the order in which one receives these three important sacraments has sparked much debate and discussion within the Catholic Church. Church officials and scholars are striving to clarify even the meaning and purpose of modern-day confirmation. Is it more a sacrament of initiation, or more a sacrament of commitment? Discussion and study continue today.

Vatican II ordered that the rite of confirmation be revised so as to express more clearly the meaning and place of this sacrament in Christian life. **The new rite** emphasizes the unity between baptism, confirmation, and holy Eucharist. To show the connection between baptism and confirmation, the person to be confirmed is asked to renew his or her baptismal promises. The unity between confirmation and holy Eucharist is emphasized by the fact that confirmation ordinarily takes place within Mass. A special Mass has been provided in which all the prayers and readings are centered around the meaning of confirmation.

Another very important feature of the new rite is the emphasis on the shared responsibility of the local parish or community in the celebration of confirmation. No longer is this sacrament to be considered an individual matter, of interest only to the persons confirmed and to their sponsors and families. **The whole People of God**, represented by the local community, is invited to take part and rejoice in the bestowal of the gift of the Holy Spirit upon its members.

LA CONFIRMACIÓN para adolescentes

CONFIRMATION for teens

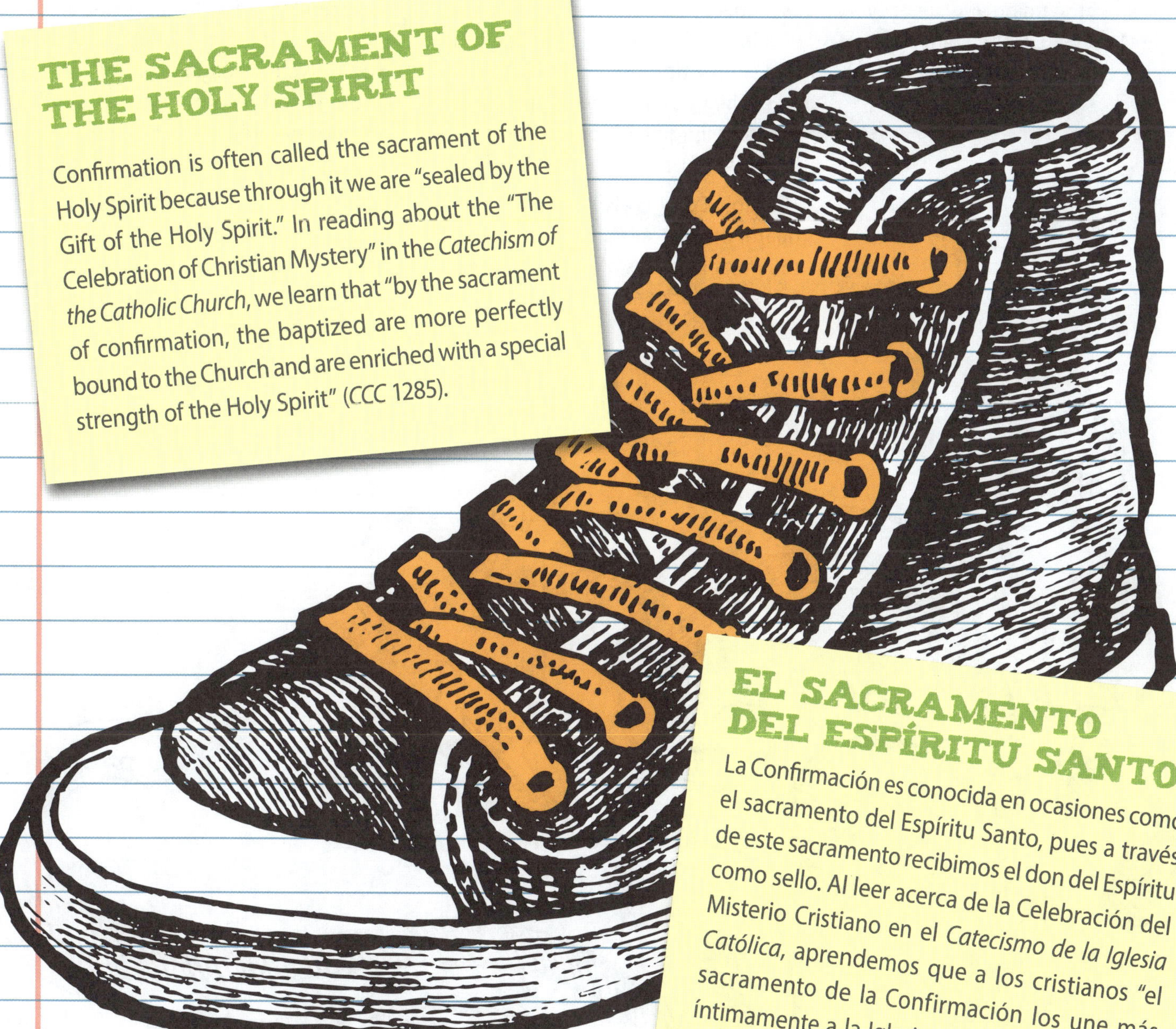

THE SACRAMENT OF THE HOLY SPIRIT

Confirmation is often called the sacrament of the Holy Spirit because through it we are "sealed by the Holy Spirit." In reading about the "The Gift of the Holy Spirit." In reading about the "The Celebration of Christian Mystery" in the *Catechism of the Catholic Church*, we learn that "by the sacrament of confirmation, the baptized are more perfectly bound to the Church and are enriched with a special strength of the Holy Spirit" (CCC 1285).

EL SACRAMENTO DEL ESPÍRITU SANTO

La Confirmación es conocida en ocasiones como el sacramento del Espíritu Santo, pues a través de este sacramento recibimos el don del Espíritu como sello. Al leer acerca de la Celebración del Misterio Cristiano en el *Catecismo de la Iglesia Católica*, aprendemos que a los cristianos "el sacramento de la Confirmación los une más íntimamente a la Iglesia y los enriquece con la fuerza especial del Espíritu Santo" (CIC 1285).

LESSON 6 DEBBIE REPP LECCIÓN 6

In the sacrament of confirmation, special emphasis is placed on the presence of the Holy Spirit in our lives and in the life of the community. It is important for us, therefore, to review what the Church treasures concerning the Holy Spirit.

Our *Catechism* has much to teach regarding the power of the Spirit. We learn that the Holy Spirit rules, sanctifies, and animates all creation. "The Word of God and his Breath are at the origin of the being and life of every creature" (*CCC* 703). The Spirit awakens our faith, enables communication with Christ (*CCC* 683-684), helps us to grow in spiritual freedom (*CCC* 1742), is the master and source of prayer (*CCC* 741, 2652), and is the "principal author" of holy Scripture (*CCC* 304). Through the power of the Holy Spirit, God is revealed to us, as is the mystery of the Trinity (*CCC* 244, 684, 687). The Church, in fact, regards the Holy Spirit as **the source of all holiness** (*CCC* 749).

Regarding our Church communities, the *Catechism* teaches that the Spirit is essential in unifying the Church (*CCC* 813) and is responsible for directing and supporting the Church (*CCC* 747, 768). The Church is the temple, the very dwelling place, of the Spirit (*CCC* 797-98).

The Holy Spirit is also a generous bearer of gifts (*CCC* 2003). One of the great benefits of receiving the sacrament of confirmation is that it **"increases the gifts of the Holy Spirit in us"** (*CCC* 1303). We will take a closer look at the gifts and fruits of the Holy Spirit in the next lesson. For now, let's examine what happens when we are "sealed by the Gift of the Holy Spirit" during confirmation.

The *Catechism of the Catholic Church* firmly states that confirmation is a celebration of "Christian mystery" in which those being confirmed receive "the full outpouring of the Holy Spirit as once granted to the apostles on the day of Pentecost" (*CCC* 1302). But once we receive this magnificent gift, we assume great responsibility, as did the apostles before us.

Carefully read the excerpts from the *Catechism* concerning the effects of confirmation. Hopefully, you will get a better idea of why confirmation is considered the *active* part of the initiation process.

En el sacramento de la Confirmación, se pone un especial énfasis en la presencia del Espíritu Santo en nuestras vidas y en la vida de la comunidad. Por tanto, es importante para nosotros repasar lo que la Iglesia enseña acerca del Espíritu Santo.

Nuestro Catecismo tiene muchas enseñanzas acerca del poder del Espíritu. Aprendemos que el Espíritu anima toda la Creación y está "en el origen del ser y de la vida de toda creatura" (*CIC* 703). El Espíritu despierta nuestra fe y permite nuestra comunicación con Cristo (*CIC* 683-684), nos ayuda a crecer en libertad espiritual (*CIC* 1742), es el maestro y fuente de la oración (*CIC* 741, 2652), y es el autor principal de la Sagrada Escritura (*CIC* 304). Por medio del poder del Espíritu Santo, se nos revela Dios, al igual que el misterio de la Trinidad (*CIC* 244, 684, 687). En efecto, la Iglesia considera al Espíritu Santo **la fuente de toda santidad** (*CIC* 749).

En lo que respecta a las comunidades de la Iglesia, el Catecismo nos enseña que el Espíritu es esencial en la unidad de la Iglesia (*CIC* 813) y que es el responsable de dirigir y apoyar a la Iglesia (*CIC* 747, 768). La Iglesia es el Templo, el lugar donde mora el Espíritu (*CIC* 797-798).

El Espíritu Santo es también el portador generoso de dones (*CIC* 2003). Uno de los beneficios más grandes de recibir el sacramento de la Confirmación es que **"aumenta en nosotros los dones del Espíritu Santo"** (*CIC* 1303). En la siguiente lección veremos con más detalle los dones y frutos del Espíritu Santo. Por ahora, examinemos lo que sucede durante la Confirmación cuando recibimos el sello del don del Espíritu Santo.

El Catecismo de la Iglesia Católica declara firmemente que la Confirmación es una celebración del misterio cristiano, en el que aquellos que van a ser confirmados, reciben "la efusión especial del Espíritu Santo, como fue concedida en otro tiempo a los Apóstoles el día de Pentecostés" (*CIC* 1302). Pero, una vez que recibimos este magnífico don, aceptamos una gran responsabilidad, del mismo modo que los Apóstoles antes que nosotros. **Lee cuidadosamente** los extractos del Catecismo que hacen referencia a los efectos de la Confirmación. Ojalá que te puedas formar una mejor idea de por qué la Confirmación se considera una parte activa del proceso de iniciación.

The Catholic Church's tremendous reverence for the Holy Spirit is rooted in sacred Scripture. The authors of Genesis, the first book of the Old Testament, were aware of the Spirit's indescribable creative power, and they refer to this power in the first passage of Scripture: "In the beginning when God created the heavens and the earth, the earth was a formless void and darkness covered the face of the deep, while **a wind from God swept over the face of the waters**" (Genesis 1:1-2).

In the Hebrew vocabulary, there is one word, *RUAH*, which means "wind," "breath," and "spirit." The different English translations vary mainly in reference to how they interpret the word, but in all translations, this Scripture verse tells us that the creative power of the Holy Spirit *was present and active at the beginning of creation.*

The word *RUAH* again appears in Genesis 2:7: "The Lord God formed man from the dust of the ground, and breathed into his nostrils the *breath* of life; and the man became a living being." The spirit of God is as close to us as our very own breath! **God indeed made us in God's own image and likeness**—and then breathed into us *the divine life and spirit!*

The Spirit that hovered over the waters at the beginning of creation also hovered over Jesus, and remained his inspiration throughout his public life. In Luke's Gospel, Jesus tells us:

"THE SPIRIT OF THE LORD IS UPON ME, BECAUSE HE HAS ANOINTED ME TO BRING GOOD NEWS TO THE POOR. HE HAS SENT ME TO PROCLAIM RELEASE TO THE CAPTIVES AND RECOVERY OF SIGHT TO THE BLIND, TO LET THE OPPRESSED GO FREE, TO PROCLAIM THE YEAR OF THE LORD'S FAVOR."

LUKE 4:18-19

JESUS does not send us out into the world to do HIS work alone. In confirmation, we are sealed with *the same Holy Spirit.* In confirmation, we celebrate our acceptance of the gift of the Spirit of Jesus and we commit ourselves to become positive, active members of his Church.

CCC 1303: From this fact, Confirmation brings an increase and deepening of baptismal grace:

- it roots us more deeply in the divine filiation which makes us cry, "Abba! Father!";
- it unites us more firmly to Christ;
- it increases the gifts of the Holy Spirit in us;
- it renders our bond with the Church more perfect;
- it gives us a special strength of the Holy Spirit to spread and defend the faith by word and action as true witnesses of Christ, to confess the name of Christ boldly, and never to be ashamed of the Cross.

CCC 1304: Like Baptism which it completes, Confirmation is given only once, for it too imprints on the soul an *indelible spiritual mark,* the "character," which is the sign that Jesus Christ has marked a Christian with the seal of his Spirit by clothing him [or her] with power from on high so that he [or she] may be his witness.

La Confirmación para adolescentes

Confirmation for teens

HOLY SPIRIT

Bearer of gifts

In the Catholic Tradition, the celebration of confirmation is closely associated with receiving the gifts of the Holy Spirit. In the Book of Isaiah (11:2-3), the great prophet describes these unique and marvelous gifts:

"The spirit of the Lord
shall rest on him,
the spirit of wisdom
and understanding,
the spirit of counsel and might,
the spirit of knowledge
and the fear of the Lord.
His delight shall be
in the fear of the Lord."

In this passage, the prophet Isaiah indicated the gifts that would be possessed by "the Messiah." These verses also teach us what special qualities the followers of Jesus receive when they are gifted with his Holy Spirit. During the sacrament of confirmation, when we are signed with the gift of the Holy Spirit, we receive the same gifts that our Messiah, Jesus Christ, possessed. What great plans our God must have for us!

EL ESPÍRITU SANTO

Portador de dones

En la Tradición católica, la celebración de la Confirmación está asociada con la recepción de los dones del Espíritu Santo. En el libro de Isaías 11:2-3, el gran profeta describe estos maravillosos y singulares dones:

"Sobre él reposará el Espíritu de Yavé,
Espíritu de sabiduría e inteligencia,
Espíritu de prudencia y valentía,
Espíritu para conocer a Yavé y para respetarlo,
y para gobernar según sus preceptos".

En este pasaje, el profeta Isaías señala los dones que el Mesías poseerá. Estos versículos nos enseñan también las cualidades especiales que los seguidores de Jesús reciben cuando poseen los dones del Espíritu Santo.

Durante el sacramento de la Confirmación, cuando somos marcados con los dones del Espíritu Santo, recibimos los mismos dones que nuestro Mesías, Jesucristo, poseyó. ¡Qué plan tan grande ha de tener Dios trazado para cada uno de nosotros!

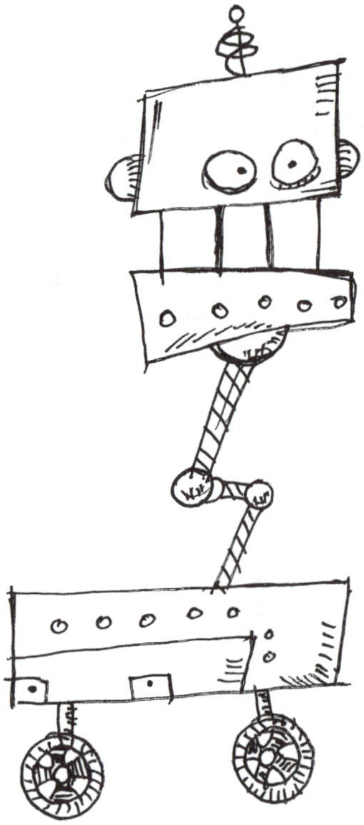

THE MEANING OF THE GIFTS OF THE HOLY SPIRIT

Let's look at each of these seven gifts and reflect upon what they mean in our present lives:

COURAGE (FORTITUDE)

is the gift that enables a person to live up to the decision he or she has made, no matter what obstacles emerge. Courage is especially valuable to young people who must continually face the challenge of remaining true to their convictions, despite the tremendous influence of peers, the media, etc.

REVERENCE (PIETY)

teaches a person to treasure and respect life and all that sustains it. The gift of reverence enables us to treat all creation with tenderness, care, and respect, just as loving parents would treat their precious children.

RIGHT JUDGMENT (COUNSEL)

means making good decisions. In order to make good decisions, one needs to do the necessary background work, understand all alternatives, and have knowledge of the consequences. Good decision-making is often difficult, and right judgment usually involves both the intellect and the heart.

WISDOM

is the opposite of narrow-mindedness. A wise person does not look at things from just one point of view, but sees the whole picture. The wise person sees things from all sides and possesses great vision.

UNDERSTANDING

means "heart-knowledge." To understand means to be able to "walk in another's shoes" and to see a situation through another's eyes. Understanding requires great sensitivity toward others' feelings and awareness of others' life experiences.

KNOWLEDGE

is the gift of thinking clearly, intelligently, and perceptively.

WONDER AND AWE IN GOD'S PRESENCE (FEAR OF THE LORD)

is the gift that allows us to recognize, with a profound feeling of amazement, that we are always in God's presence. This gift enables a person to experience all of life as a great gift given by God and to recognize God's presence in every individual.

SIGNIFICADO DE LOS DONES DEL ESPÍRITU SANTO

Veamos cada uno de los siete dones y reflexionemos acerca de su significado en nuestras vidas:

PIEDAD

Enseña a la persona a guardar y respetar la vida, y todo aquello que la sostiene. El don de la piedad nos permite tratar a toda la creación con ternura, cuidado y respeto, así como unos padres de familia cariñosos tratarían a sus hijos.

FORTALEZA

Es el don que permite a la persona vivir de acuerdo con las decisiones que ha tomado, sin importar los obstáculos que se le presenten. La fortaleza es algo muy valioso para aquellos jóvenes que están enfrentando a diario el reto de permanecer firmes en sus convicciones, a pesar de la tremenda influencia de los compañeros, de los medios de comunicación, etc.

SABIDURÍA

Es lo contrario de una mente cerrada. Una persona sabia no ve las situaciones desde una sola perspectiva, sino que las ve desde todos los ángulos posibles y posee una visión muy amplia de la realidad.

CONSEJO

Significa tomar buenas decisiones. Para tomar buenas decisiones, uno necesita llevar a cabo un trabajo previo, entender todas las alternativas posibles y poseer conocimiento de todas las consecuencias. Tomar buenas decisiones es algo difícil y esto requiere normalmente inteligencia y corazón.

SANTO TEMOR

Es el don que nos permite reconocer, con un profundo sentimiento de asombro, que estamos continuamente en la presencia de Dios. Este don le permite a la persona experimentar la vida en su totalidad, como un gran don de Dios, y a reconocer, al mismo tiempo, la presencia de Dios en cada individuo.

INTELIGENCIA

Hace referencia al conocimiento del corazón. "Entender" significa ser capaz de ponerse en el lugar del otro y ver la situación como la ve la otra persona. Entender al otro requiere una gran sensibilidad para comprender los sentimientos y ser consciente de las experiencias de vida de las demás personas.

CIENCIA

es el don por el cual uno piensa con inteligencia, de modo claro y perceptivo.

During the confirmation ceremony, the bishop extends his hands over the candidates and prays:

"All-powerful God,
Father of our Lord Jesus Christ,
by water and the Holy Spirit
you freed your sons and daughters from
sin and gave them new life.
Send your Holy Spirit upon them
to be their helper and guide.
Give them the spirit of wisdom
and understanding, the spirit
of right judgment and courage,
the spirit of knowledge and reverence.
Fill them with the
spirit of wonder and awe
in your presence.
We ask this through
Christ our Lord."

WHY DOES THE SPIRIT GIVE US THESE GIFTS?

The *Catechism of the Catholic Church* makes some interesting points in its description of the gifts of the Holy Spirit. First, it tells us that the gifts "belong in their fullness to Christ" (*CCC* 1831). In other words, as we actively make use of these gifts, we become more Christlike. Secondly, the *Catechism* explains that the gifts of the Holy Spirit "complete and perfect the virtues of those who receive them" (*CCC* 1831). This statement implies that God creates us full of goodness and virtue—indeed in the divine image and likeness—and the Spirit helps us to develop and perfect our goodness through these gifts, "For all who are led by the Spirit of God are children of God" (Romans 8:14).

Another important point must be made about the gifts of the Holy Spirit. These gifts are not granted just for the happiness of the person who receives them. They are given *for the good of your entire parish, for the good of the whole Church, and the good of the entire world.* The gifts of the Holy Spirit are given to build up the Body of Christ and to make it holy. The Body of Christ is made holy because these gifts strengthen individual Christians to bear witness to Christ. The gifts enable the people of God to live as Jesus lived. The gifts of the Holy Spirit give us all that is needed to become active members and total participants in Christian life.

THE FRUITS OF THE HOLY SPIRIT

In Saint Paul's Letter to the Galatians, we read: "The fruit of the spirit is love, joy, peace, patience, kindness, generosity, faithfulness, gentleness and self-control" (5:22-23). In other words, when we actively immerse ourselves in the building of God's kingdom on earth, we will reap the "fruits" of our hard work and personal growth. Using Scripture as a reference, the Church has traditionally taught twelve fruits of the Holy Spirit. They are "charity, joy, peace, patience, kindness, goodness, generosity, gentleness, faith, modesty, self-control, and chastity (appropriate use of our gift of sexuality)" (*CCC* 1832).

When we are sealed with the gift of the Holy Spirit, we begin a new journey of growth toward Christian maturity. With the help of the Spirit's gifts, we can live full human and Christian lives and become loving, humble, peace-filled people.

La Confirmación para adolescentes

Confirmation for teens

A Sacrament of Christian Witness

Jesus spent the first 30 years of his life as an "unknown" in a small country town quietly practicing his trade. When he began his public ministry—preaching about the kingdom of God—he was baptized by his cousin John in the Jordan River. There, a marvelous thing happened. Jesus was "confirmed" in his mission on earth.

Un sacramento de testimonio cristiano

Jesús pasó los primeros treinta años de su vida trabajando como un desconocido en una aldea pequeña y callada. Cuando comenzó su ministerio público, predicando acerca del Reino de Dios, fue bautizado por su primo Juan en el río Jordán. Ahí sucedió un gran acontecimiento: Jesús fue confirmado en su misión terrena.

When the bishop seals you with the Holy Spirit, you will be confirmed with the same Spirit Luke spoke of in his Gospel:

"When all the people were baptized, and when Jesus also had been baptized and was praying, **the heaven was opened**, and the Holy Spirit descended upon him in bodily form like a dove. And a voice came from heaven, 'You are my Son, the Beloved; with you I am well pleased'" (3:21-22).

Later that day, according to Luke, Jesus went to the desert to spend time fasting and praying. He pondered what his call meant and how he was to fulfill his mission. Jesus spent time alone, trying to understand what the Father's will was for him. Through sincere prayer, quiet reflection, and the power of the Spirit, Jesus returned to Nazareth prepared to dedicate his life to spreading the Good News. In other words, even Jesus had to journey toward self-discovery. He had to ask himself the same questions you are asking yourself now.

Jesus publicly announced his mission by reading a portion from Isaiah that prophesied the Messiah's mission on earth:

"**The Spirit of the Lord is upon me,**
because he has anointed me
to bring good news to the poor.
He has sent me to proclaim release
to the captives
and recovery of sight to the blind,
to let the oppressed go free,
to proclaim the year of the
Lord's favor.

Then Jesus rolled up the scroll, sat down, and said to those gathered there waiting, 'Today this scripture has been is fulfilled in your hearing'" (Luke 4:18-19,21).

CHRISTIAN WITNESS

A Commitment to Do the Work of Jesus

It is the mission of the entire Church to do Jesus's work so that the kingdom of God can become a reality on earth as it is in heaven.
Just imagine what a marvelous planet it would be if the poor received what they needed; and if those who were imprisoned by fear or hatred were released from that bondage; and if those blinded by ignorance or prejudice could begin to see every human being as worthy of respect and kindness. Truly, **this would be heaven on earth**!

To make the reign of God real on earth, every confirmed Christian individually and the Church as a community must be committed to the mission prophesied by Isaiah and so strongly acknowledged by Jesus.

On the day of your confirmation, you will be "sealed by the Gift of the Holy Spirit." You will commit yourself to the mission of Jesus. In your own unique way, however great or small, you will be expected "to bring good news to the poor, to proclaim release to the captives, and recovery of sight to the blind." The mission of our Lord Jesus will become your mission, too.

While confirmation is first a sacrament of initiation, recall that it is the active part of the initiation process. Adolescent confirmation, in particular, usually includes an element of Christian witness—a commitment to do the work of Jesus by becoming more fully involved in the life of the Church. Parishes vary in the degree to which they emphasize the "service" aspect of confirmation, but it is important to understand **what it means to share in the mission of Jesus**.

Cuando el obispo te selle con el don del Espíritu Santo, serás confirmado con el mismo Espíritu que Lucas menciona en su Evangelio:

"Un día fue bautizado también Jesús entre el pueblo que venía a recibir el Bautismo. Y mientras estaba en oración, **se abrieron los cielos**: el Espíritu Santo bajó sobre él y se manifestó exteriormente en forma de paloma, y del cielo vino una voz: 'Tú eres mi Hijo, hoy te he dado a la vida'" (Lc 3:21-22).

Más tarde en ese mismo día, Lucas nos dice que Jesús se fue al desierto y ahí pasó un tiempo de ayuno y oración. Ponderó lo que su misión significaba y cómo la iba a realizar. **Pasó tiempo solo**, tratando de entender cuál era la voluntad de su Padre para Él. Por medio de una oración sincera, de una reflexión silenciosa y del poder del Espíritu Santo, Jesús regresó a Nazaret preparado para dedicar su vida a propagar la Buena Nueva. Dicho de otro modo, Jesús también tuvo que recorrer el camino de conocerse a sí mismo. Él también tuvo que hacerse las mismas preguntas que tú te estás haciendo en este momento.

Jesús anunció públicamente su misión con la lectura de una parte del libro de Isaías, en la que profetiza acerca de la misión del Mesías en la tierra:

"**El Espíritu del Señor está sobre mí**. Él me ha ungido para llevar buenas noticias a los pobres, para anunciar la libertad a los cautivos y a los ciegos que pronto van a ver, para poner en libertad a los oprimidos y proclamar el año de gracia del Señor.

Jesús entonces enrolló el libro, lo devolvió al ayudante y se sentó, y empezó a decirles: 'Hoy se cumplen estas palabras proféticas y a ustedes les llegan noticias de ello'" (Lc 4:18-19,21).

TESTIMONIO CRISTIANO

Un compromiso para realizar la obra de Jesús

Es la misión de la Iglesia entera realizar la obra de Jesús para que el Reino de Dios pueda ser una realidad en la Tierra, del mismo modo como lo es en el Cielo. Solo imagina lo maravilloso que sería el mundo si los pobres recibieran lo que necesitan; si aquellos que están encarcelados por miedo u odio, fueran liberados de esas cadenas; si quienes están cegados por la ignorancia y el prejuicio, pudieran llegar a ver a cada ser humano como digno de respeto y amor. En verdad **esto sería el Cielo en la Tierra**.

A fin de hacer el reinado de Dios algo real en la Tierra, cada cristiano en particular y la Iglesia como comunidad, deben comprometerse a realizar la misión que Isaías profetizó y que Jesús vivió de modo tan claro.

En el día de su Confirmación ustedes serán marcados con el Don del Espíritu Santo. Se comprometerán a realizar la obra de Jesús. Se espera que cada uno, a su modo, ya sea grande o pequeño, lleve la Buena Nueva a los pobres, proclame la libertad a los cautivos y dé la vista a los ciegos. La misión de Nuestro Señor Jesús también es tu misión.

Recuerda que la Confirmación es el primer sacramento de iniciación, a la vez que conforma la parte activa de todo el proceso de iniciación. En particular, la Confirmación de adolescentes incluye normalmente un elemento de testimonio cristiano, un compromiso de llevar a cabo la obra de Jesús por medio de la participación cada vez mayor en la vida de la Iglesia. En cada parroquia varía el grado de énfasis que se pone en el aspecto de servicio de la Confirmación. Sin embargo, es importante entender lo **que significa participar en la misión de Jesús**.

CONFIRMATION AND BEING "OF SERVICE"

So what does sharing in Jesus' mission mean for young men and women today? The gospels show us over and over that much of Jesus' mission was "service," **especially to the poor and the outcasts**.

A true servant is almost unaware of himself or herself. The needs of others become the primary focus. As disciples of Jesus, our challenge as Christian servants is to become more aware of the needs of those around us, especially the people we encounter in everyday life.

Yet, we are not *all* called to be missionaries in a foreign land. Sometimes a seemingly insignificant act of kindness may actually be a great act of service. When considering service projects as part of your preparation for confirmation, first think about the following:

What kind of personality do you have? Are you a good organizer who likes to get involved with lots of different kinds of people? Or are you a person who prefers to work one-on-one or in very small groups?

What do you enjoy doing? Service can and even should be enjoyable and rewarding. For example, if you are a computer whiz, would you enjoy tutoring other students or donating your talents to a service organization? If you love sports, would you find it rewarding to assist with coaching younger students or perhaps spend an hour a week quietly coaching a teammate who is struggling with his or her skills? If you love children, consider helping out with a baby-sitting program during Mass or entertaining little ones in your neighborhood after school.

What kind of demands do you already have on your time? The purpose of a service project is not to add stress to your life or the lives of your parents. Consider ideas that are workable and realistic. If your life is already filled with too much activity, you might consider dropping activities that are not truly adding to the quality of your life. This in itself could be of real service to you and your family!

Consider service projects that you will want to continue after you have received the sacrament of confirmation. Remember, confirmation requires that we become more fully immersed in the life of the Church. We must **change our hearts** and become young men and women who lead lives of service—not when it is convenient, but rather when it is needed.

The wonderful thing about service is that rewards are tremendous. **When we serve, we love;** we become less self-absorbed, and less focused on our own wants. Eventually following a path of loving service becomes a way of life. People who serve are joy and peace-filled individuals who, in their service, come to see the face of God.

LA CONFIRMACIÓN
para adolescentes

CONFIRMATION for teens

SIGNS AND SYMBOLS OF THE SACRAMENT OF CONFIRMATION

Think about what it's like to wake up late and begin your day in a rush. You jump out of bed and look at the clock, knowing that you've overslept. You barely have time to brush your teeth, throw on your clothes, and gather your school papers before your ride arrives. A moment later, you're out the door, a glass of juice, and your schoolbooks in hand. Your carpool has only been waiting a minute or so…You've made it!

SIGNOS Y SÍMBOLOS DEL SACRAMENTO DE LA CONFIRMACIÓN

Piensa lo qué sería levantarte tarde y comenzar tu día a la carrera. Te levantaste de la cama y viste el reloj. Sabes que se te hizo tarde. Apenas tienes tiempo para lavarte los dientes, ponerte la ropa y tomar todos tus útiles escolares antes de que pasen a recogerte. Un momento después, ya estás fuera de casa con un vaso de jugo de naranja en la mano y tu mochila a la espalda. Solo han estado esperándote un minuto, ¡lo has logrado!

Now you can relax. You're back on schedule. Right?

Perhaps not. As the morning passes, you never seem to catch up. You begin to think that you should have never gotten out of bed. **Nothing seems to go smoothly.** Nothing seems quite "right." You feel out of synch with everything going on around you. What is happening here? You feel so out of it.

Part of the reason for your disorientation is the stress late rising caused. Stress always affects one's outlook and state of mind. Another explanation is that you broke your normal morning "rising rite." You did not follow your usual routine—and that caused a problem. Without our usual patterns of doing things, we feel awkward and disoriented.

Now think a moment about the ways in which your family celebrates Christmas. Chances are, each person in your class has special "happenings" and traditions unique to his or her own family. **No two families decorate their trees quite the same.** Some families exchange gifts on Christmas Eve, others on Christmas morning. Some love the tradition of attending Midnight Mass. Others like to celebrate the Eucharist on Christmas morning. However you celebrate this glorious holy day, your family's traditions feel "just right," and if you did not have them, Christmas would not be quite the same.

So what do the morning rising ritual and Christmas traditions have to do with the celebration of the sacrament of confirmation? In a word—RITUAL. Much of your day is made up of ritual, and these procedures play a big part in how you effectively get things done. They make you feel comfortable with the important tasks you have to fulfill. Most people have a regular way that they get out of bed, wash their faces, and prepare for the day. They go through these steps quite routinely. Their ritual is second nature to them. At Christmas, you know where you like to place the tree and all the other important symbols of the season. Again, **your family's Christmas rituals are second nature to you**.

All of the rituals and symbols of daily life join together to make life meaningful and predictable. They are necessary for the healthy functioning of an individual each day.

Each of our sacraments also has a specific pattern and procedure that is peculiar to it. Because the sacrament of confirmation is contained within a ritual, understanding the symbols in the confirmation rite is important. It is the liturgical celebration that externally expresses the faith and commitment present within the community. The celebration points to God's action in the lives of the worshiping community.

There are nine significant signs of the presence of God in the celebration of the sacrament of confirmation:

- The Christian community assembled
- The bishop
- The candidates
- The sponsors
- The Word of God
- The prayer of the community for the gift of the Spirit
- The laying on of hands
- The anointing with chrism
- The Eucharist

A "sign" or "symbol" is something perceived by the senses that represents something deeper. For instance, we often use the "sign of the cross" to represent our faith in the Trinity. We further talk about the cross being a symbol of Christianity. When we refer to the signs in the confirmation ritual, we are referring to physical, concrete realities that stand for the more important abstract realities of our faith. **Let's examine some of these signs.**

Ahora puedes tranquilizarte. Ya vas con el horario, ¿no es así? Quizá no. A medida que la mañana transcurre, pareciera que no te acomodas al horario. Comienzas a pensar que hubiera sido bueno nunca haberte levantado de la cama. **Nada parece ser normal.** Nada parece ir bien. Te sientes fuera de contexto con todo aquello que sucede a tu alrededor. ¿Qué es lo que está pasando? Te sientes tan extraño.

Parte de la causa por la que te sientes desorientado, es el estrés que te causó levantarte tarde. El estrés siempre afecta nuestra visión y estado de ánimo. Otra explicación es que rompiste con el "rito de levantarte" que normalmente tienes. No comenzaste con la rutina normal y eso causó problemas. Si no seguimos nuestro modo normal de hacer las cosas, nos sentimos raros y desorientados.

Ahora tómate un tiempo para pensar cómo celebra la Navidad tu familia. Es probable que cada persona en tu salón tenga un modo único y especial de celebrar las tradiciones navideñas en su familia. **No existen dos familias que adornen del mismo modo sus árboles de Navidad.** Algunas familias reparten los regalos durante la noche de Navidad, otras familias durante la mañana de Navidad. Algunos aman la tradición de escuchar Misa de media noche. Otros prefieren la celebración del día de Navidad. De la manera en que celebres estas festividades, las tradiciones de la familia nos hacen sentir bien. Si no guardáramos esas tradiciones, la Navidad no sería la misma.

Entonces, ¿qué tienen que ver el rito de levantarse por la mañana y las tradiciones navideñas con la celebración del sacramento de la Confirmación? Una sola palabra: RITUAL. La mayor parte de tu día es un ritual y este modo de proceder tiene un papel muy importante en la efectividad con la que realizas tus deberes. Te hace sentir tranquilo con todas las tareas importantes que tienes que realizar. La mayoría de la gente tiene un modo particular de levantarse de la cama, de lavarse la cara y de prepararse para el día. La gente recorre estos pasos con cierta rutina. Para estas personas, sus ritos son una segunda naturaleza. Para la Navidad, ya sabes dónde te gusta colocar el árbol y todos aquellos símbolos que tienen que ver con esta temporada. Una vez más, **los ritos que sigue tu familia durante la Navidad son una segunda naturaleza para ti**.

Todos los ritos y símbolos de la vida diaria se unen para dar a nuestra vida algo de sentido y hacerla algo predecible. Son necesarios para el correcto funcionamiento de la persona, día a día.

Cada uno de nuestros sacramentos tiene un patrón específico y un procedimiento que le es peculiar. Dado que el sacramento de la Confirmación está dentro de un ritual, entender los símbolos del rito de la Confirmación es algo sumamente importante. La Celebración litúrgica es la que expresa externamente la fe y el compromiso presente dentro de la comunidad. La celebración apunta a la acción de Dios en la vida de la comunidad que da culto.

Existen nueve signos importantes de la presencia de Dios en la celebración del sacramento de la Confirmación:

- La asamblea de la comunidad cristiana
- El obispo
- Los candidatos
- Los padrinos
- La Palabra de Dios
- La oración de la comunidad pidiendo los dones del Espíritu Santo
- La imposición de las manos
- La unción con el crisma
- La Eucaristía

Un signo o símbolo es algo que percibimos por medio de los sentidos y que representa algo más profundo. Por ejemplo, nosotros hacemos continuamente el signo de la cruz para representar nuestra fe en la Trinidad. Además, hablamos de la cruz siendo este un símbolo del cristianismo. Cuando nos referimos a los signos en el rito de la Confirmación, hacemos referencia a realidades físicas y concretas que están ahí en lugar de las realidades abstractas más importantes de nuestra fe. **Examinemos algunos de estos signos.**

THE CHRISTIAN COMMUNITY ASSEMBLED

When the community gathers together in faith, the gathering is the Church of Jesus Christ. When this group of believers is together, they recall the teachings and life of their Lord, and especially his promise to be present when two or more are gathered in his name. The community is the kingdom of God on earth. The challenge of the sacrament is for the community to continue the kingdom and to spread it "on earth, as it is in heaven."

Sacraments are expressions of the faith of the community. In the community, the Spirit comes, and with the gifts given by the Spirit, the community witnesses and shares Jesus' mission with the whole world. Confirmation is a celebration that renews and enlivens the whole Christian community.

THE BISHOP

The bishop is the spiritual leader of the local Church and a link to the universal Church. He symbolizes the unity between the parish community and the universal Church. Together with the priests and deacons, the bishop ministers to the diocesan community and to each parish in that community. He has the primary responsibility for ensuring that the life of the Spirit is properly celebrated. The bishop also has ultimate responsibility for discerning the gifts of the Spirit as they unfold in the life of the local Church. Together with the other bishops, he represents the apostles in their role of continuing the Church of Jesus Christ.

CANDIDATES FOR CONFIRMATION

You, as a candidate for confirmation, are a sign, too. You are a sign of the gift of the Spirit as it unfolds in your own individual life, a sign of hope and renewal for the entire Christian community.

You are celebrating a special moment in your process of growth into a fuller Christian life, a life that will be a unique manifestation of the Spirit alive today.

THE SPONSORS

The sponsor is a symbol of the adult Christian community and is a representative of that adult community. Your sponsor should be your godparent, if possible, to emphasize the unity between the sacraments of baptism and confirmation. Otherwise, you should choose someone who can actually accompany and assist you in unfolding the gift of the Spirit in your life, a person who will help you bring this gift to maturity in the Christian community.

THE WORD OF GOD

The reading of Scripture is an important element of the confirmation liturgy because it is a sign of "the many-sided power of the Holy Spirit which flows upon the Church and upon each one of the baptized and confirmed, and it is by this word that God's will is manifest in the life of Christians" (Rite of Confirmation, 13).

The phrase, "the Word of God," is itself a verbal symbol of Jesus' teaching, life, and message. Therefore, the reading of Scripture during the confirmation celebration is, in effect, the reading of the mission of Christ, the basis of the faith of you who are being confirmed.

THE PRAYER OF THE COMMUNITY

When the Christian community, led by the bishop, prays for the gift of the Holy Spirit, the community is signifying its dependence upon the Father, through Jesus, for the gift of the Spirit. The community gathered with you, led by the bishop, recognizes its need to be open to the Spirit and, through that recognition, expresses the community's faith in the goodness of the Father to give you all you need to live out the mission of Jesus.

THE LAYING ON OF HANDS

The laying on of hands is an important biblical gesture by which the Holy Spirit is asked to come to you. In the gospels, Jesus healed many people with a touch. One time, he even mentioned that when a woman with a hemorrhage touched his cloak with the intention of being healed, he experienced power going out from himself.

Today there is a lot of information that indicates touching is a significant act, which brings life and healing to the person being touched. It makes sense that the power of the Holy Spirit is invoked with the laying on of hands and praying for the gift of the Spirit for you.

THE ANOINTING WITH CHRISM

The gift of the Spirit is actually conferred on you through the laying on of hands and the anointing with chrism on your forehead as the bishop says: "Be sealed with the Gift of the Holy Spirit." Chrism, an oil that is blessed by the bishop, is a sign of the priesthood of Christ to which we are all called through our baptism.

THE EUCHARIST

An especially appropriate context for the celebration of confirmation is within the eucharistic liturgy. The Eucharist is the sign of Christ's way of life. It is, therefore, a sign of your own death and resurrection journey. The Eucharist signifies the "oneness" of the entire Church in Jesus Christ and acknowledges our mission to work for the kingdom.

These signs and symbols constantly challenge us to live fuller Christian lives. Seek to unfold the meaning of the Spirit in your life through prayer and a constant pursuit of answers to your religious and spiritual questions. You will then discover that this confirmation celebration will be the "little Pentecost" it is meant to be.

LA CONFIRMACIÓN para adolescentes

CONFIRMATION for teens

CELEBRATION OF THE RITE OF CONFIRMATION

One of the best ways to grow in appreciation and understanding of the sacrament of confirmation is to look at the Rite of Confirmation itself. There we see the points emphasized by the Church.

LA CELEBRACIÓN DEL RITO DE LA CONFIRMACIÓN

Una de las mejores formas de crecer en la apreciación y comprensión del sacramento de la Confirmación es mirar al rito mismo de la Confirmación. Ahí es donde vemos los puntos que resalta la Iglesia.

LESSON 10

DEBBIE REPP

LECCIÓN 10

THE GATHERING AND ENTRANCE

The celebration of the sacrament of confirmation begins by getting all the participants into their places. This is the purpose of the entrance procession. It is a solemn moment that sets the tone for all that is to follow. Usually, the procession includes the crossbearer and acolytes, the candidates for confirmation and their sponsors, the lector who carries in the Word of God, the deacon, the presider(s), and the bishop. The entire assembly sings an appropriate song during this time, establishing an atmosphere of prayer and celebration.

LITURGY OF THE WORD

The Liturgy of the Word is the proclamation of the readings from Sacred Scriptures. These readings, which can be found in the Lectionary, should be studied in advance by the candidates.

THE INSTRUCTION

After the gospel, the candidates for confirmation are presented to the bishop. The bishop then delivers an instructional homily in these or similar words:

> ***On the day of Pentecost*** *the apostles received the Holy Spirit as the Lord had promised. They also received the power of giving the Holy Spirit to others and so completing the work of baptism. This we read in the Acts of the Apostles. When Saint Paul placed his hands on those who had been baptized, the Holy Spirit came upon them, and they began to speak in other languages and in prophetic words.*
>
> ***Bishops are successors of the apostles*** *and have this power of giving the Holy Spirit to the baptized, either personally or through the priests they appoint.*
>
> *In our day, the coming of the Holy Spirit in confirmation is no longer marked by the gift of tongues; we know the Spirit's coming by faith. The Spirit fills our hearts with the love of God, brings us together in one faith but in different vocations, and works within us to make the Church one and holy.*
>
> ***The gift of the Holy Spirit*** *which you are to receive will be a spiritual sign and seal to make you more like Christ and to challenge you to become more active members of his Church. At his baptism by John, Christ himself was anointed by the Spirit and sent out on his public ministry.*
>
> *You have already been baptized into Christ, and now you will receive the power of his Spirit and the sign of the cross on your forehead. You must be witnesses before all the world to his suffering, death, and resurrection; your way of life should at all times reflect the goodness of Christ. Christ gives varied gifts to his Church, and the Spirit distributes them among the members of Christ's body to build up the holy people of God in unity and love.*
>
> ***Be active members of the Church****, alive in Jesus Christ. Under the guidance of the Holy Spirit give your lives completely in the service of all, as did Christ, who came not to be served but to serve (from the Rite of Confirmation).*

After all have been instructed by the bishop, the candidates renew their baptismal promises by rejecting Satan and professing their faith in the Lord and the Church. In this way, the candidates are reminded that confirmation completes the sacraments of initiation. They accept the Christian way of life as their own.

LA ASAMBLEA Y LA ENTRADA

La celebración del sacramento de la Confirmación inicia con la reunión de todos los participantes en sus lugares. Este es el fin de la procesión de entrada. Es un momento solemne que marca el tono para todo lo que viene enseguida. Normalmente, la procesión incluye al crucífero y a los acólitos, los candidatos y sus padrinos, el lector que porta la Palabra de Dios, el diácono, el o los concelebrantes y el obispo. Toda la asamblea entona un canto apropiado durante la procesión, estableciendo así una atmósfera de oración y celebración.

LITURGIA DE LA PALABRA

La Liturgia de la Palabra es la proclamación de las lecturas de la Sagrada Escritura. Estas lecturas pueden encontrarse en el leccionario. Los candidatos deben estudiar por adelantado estas lecturas.

LA HOMILÍA

Después del Evangelio, los candidatos para la Confirmación son presentados al obispo. En seguida, el obispo dirige una monición con estas palabras o con otras semejantes:

> ***En el día de Pentecostés*** *los Apóstoles recibieron el Espíritu Santo como el Señor lo había prometido. También recibieron el poder de dar el Espíritu Santo a otros y de completar de este modo la obra del Bautismo. Esto lo leemos en los Hechos de los Apóstoles. Cuando san Pablo impuso sus manos en aquellos que eran bautizados, el Espíritu Santo descendía sobre ellos y comenzaban a hablar otras lenguas y palabras proféticas.*
>
> ***Los obispos son sucesores de los Apóstoles*** *y tienen el poder de conferir el Espíritu Santo a los bautizados, ya sea personalmente o por medio de los sacerdotes asignados.*
>
> *En nuestros días, la venida del Espíritu Santo durante la Confirmación ya no está acompañada por el don de lenguas; nosotros sabemos que el Espíritu viene por medio de la fe. El Espíritu llena nuestros corazones con el amor de Dios, nos une en una fe, pero en diversas vocaciones; y trabaja junto con nosotros para hacer de la Iglesia Una y Santa.*
>
> ***El don del Espíritu Santo*** *que están por recibir será un signo espiritual, un sello para hacerse más semejantes a Cristo y un desafío para volverse miembros activos de su Iglesia. Al ser bautizado por Juan, Cristo mismo fue ungido por el Espíritu y enviado a su ministerio público.*
>
> *Ustedes ya fueron bautizados en Cristo y ahora recibirán el poder de su Espíritu y el signo de la cruz en su frente. Ustedes deben ser testigos ante todo el mundo de sus sufrimientos, de su muerte y de su resurrección. Su estilo de vida debe ser en todo momento un reflejo de la bondad de Cristo. Cristo otorga dones muy variados a su Iglesia y el Espíritu Santo los distribuye entre los miembros del Cuerpo de Cristo para edificar al Pueblo Santo de Dios en unidad y amor.*
>
> ***Sean miembros activos de la Iglesia*** *que vive en Jesucristo. Bajo la guía del Espíritu Santo, den sus vidas completamente al servicio de todos, así como Cristo lo hizo, pues vino no a ser servido sino a servir (del Rito de Confirmación).*

Después de que han sido instruidos por el obispo, los candidatos renuevan sus promesas bautismales rechazando a Satanás y profesando su fe en el Señor y la Iglesia. De este modo, se les recuerda a los candidatos que la Confirmación completa los sacramentos de iniciación. Ellos aceptan el modo de vida cristiano como algo propio.

THE SACRAMENT OF CONFIRMATION

At this point, the actual sacrament of confirmation is bestowed upon the candidates, who have prepared their hearts to receive the seal of the Holy Spirit. The bishop asks the assembled community to pray for the candidates. After all have prayed in silence, the bishop lays his hands on the candidates, asking the Holy Spirit to come in power upon them. With outstretched arms, he prays:

> *All-powerful God, Father of our Lord Jesus Christ,*
> *by water and the Holy Spirit you freed your sons and daughters from sin and gave them new life.*
> *Send your Holy Spirit upon them to be their helper and guide.*
> *Give them the spirit of wisdom and understanding,*
> *the spirit of right judgment and courage, the spirit of knowledge and reverence. Fill them with the spirit of wonder and awe in your presence. We ask this through Christ our Lord. Amen*
> *(from the Rite of Confirmation)*

The oil of chrism is then brought to the bishop. **Each candidate is presented to the bishop** and stands or kneels before him. The candidate's sponsor places his or her hand on the shoulder of the candidate, and the bishop, with his thumb moistened in the sacred chrism, makes the sign of the cross on the forehead of the one to be confirmed while saying:

"N., be sealed with the Gift of the Holy Spirit."

The newly-confirmed responds: "Amen."

The bishop then gives the newly-confirmed a sign of peace, and the **parish community pledges its support** for the newly-confirmed by a sign of peace or a prayer said as a community.

THE EUCHARIST

The sacrament of confirmation is best celebrated in the context of the eucharistic liturgy. With the renewal of baptismal promises preceding confirmation and the eucharistic liturgy following, the three sacraments of initiation form a unity.

FINAL BLESSING

At the end of the liturgy, before all leave in an orderly procession, the bishop gives the assembled community a solemn blessing. This blessing completes the Rite of Confirmation:

> *God our Father made you his children by water and the Holy Spirit: may he bless you and watch over you with his fatherly love.*
>
> **Amen**
>
> *Jesus Christ the Son of God promised that the Spirit of truth would be with his Church for ever: may he bless you and give you courage in professing the true faith.*
>
> **Amen**
>
> *The Holy Spirit*
> *came down upon the disciples*
> *and set their hearts on fire with love: may he bless you, keep you one in faith and love and bring you to the joy of God's kingdom.*
>
> **Amen**
>
> The bishop adds immediately:
> *May almighty God bless you,*
> *the Father, and the Son, and the Holy Spirit.*
>
> **Amen**

La Confirmación para adolescentes

Confirmation for teens

SUMMARY, REVIEW AND SOME FINAL THOUGHTS

In the very first lesson, we spoke of the sacrament of confirmation as "food" for our great journey, that is, our spiritual journey. That part of the journey leading toward the sacrament is now coming to an end. It began with your baptism and grew in the faith community. You learned how to be a Christian not only in your religion classes, but also by seeing how other people followed the teachings of Christ. Your parents and those you love have had tremendous influence on your faith development. Your faith has been nurtured largely by those who care for you.

COMPENDIO, REPASO Y ALGUNOS ÚLTIMOS PENSAMIENTOS

En la primera lección hablamos del sacramento de la Confirmación como alimento para nuestro gran viaje, es decir, nuestro viaje espiritual. Esa parte del camino que nos lleva hacia el sacramento está llegando a su fin. Comenzó con el Bautismo y se desarrolló dentro de la comunidad de fe. Aprendiste cómo ser cristiano no solo en las clases de religión, sino también observando cómo otras personas seguían las enseñanzas de Cristo. Tus padres y tus seres queridos tuvieron un influjo considerable en el desarrollo de tu fe. Tu fe ha sido nutrida en su mayor parte por aquellos que han cuidado de ti.

LESSON 11 — DEBBIE REPP — LECCIÓN 11

Now, however, the responsibility for further faith development is shifting. The decision to receive the sacrament of confirmation is your decision. Acceptance of the sacrament of confirmation is your personal—and public—proclamation that you choose to journey in the footsteps of Jesus Christ. This is the point in your spiritual journey when you consciously and thoughtfully decide to live the mission of Christ and become more fully immersed in the life of his Church.

In the past ten lessons, the sacrament of confirmation was examined. Let's review some of the insights and understandings you have explored during this preparation time.

SPIRITUAL GROWTH IS A LIFELONG JOURNEY

You are traveling on a spiritual journey that started with your baptism toward wholeness and oneness with God. But it is not an easy journey. It is a journey that continues through hard times and challenging moments. Because you are aware of the marvelous allies you have to help you along this way of Jesus—especially the community of believers, the help of our Lord himself, and the sacraments of the Church—you will not lose hope, even when times are very difficult. You may not feel "dramatically different" after you have been confirmed, but through the grace of God, the power of the Holy Spirit, and your own deeper commitment—**you will be strengthened in faith**. Always remember though, mature Christian faith involves a lifelong journey.

THE SACRAMENTS OF INITIATION

Christians are fully incorporated into Christ through the sacraments of initiation: baptism, confirmation, and Eucharist.

In the early Church, when a person wished to fully participate in the Christian community, he or she would go through a relatively long period of study and preparation, called the "catechumenate." After this time of preparation, the "catechumen" would then receive baptism, confirmation, and the Eucharist, all in one glorious celebration at Easter.

Today, confirmation also emphasizes the individual believer's "yes" to Jesus Christ through genuine commitment to become more involved in the life of the Church.

THE HISTORY OF THE SACRAMENT OF CONFIRMATION

The sacrament of confirmation has changed throughout the centuries of the Church and even at this time the Catholic Church is striving to more clearly define **its meaning and purpose**. You explored many of these changes. You discovered that originally the sacraments of initiation—baptism, confirmation, and Eucharist—were celebrated at the Easter Vigil after a long period of preparation. (For new Catholics entering the Church who have never been baptized, the three sacraments are still celebrated in this order during the Easter Vigil.) In time, these three sacraments were separated. The babies of the Christian parents were baptized and it became the parents' responsibility to pass on the beliefs of the community to their children. The sacrament of confirmation took on a new dimension. **The newly-confirmed person now assumes much greater responsibility in his or her own faith development.**

When you receive confirmation, you will be expected to more fully contribute to the "work" of the Church—the mission that Jesus himself exercised. That participation in the life of the Church requires a rather thoughtful decision and, therefore, many bishops ask that the person seeking to be confirmed be mature enough to make this decision. Thus, in most dioceses, young men and women are confirmed sometime during their teen years.

Sin embargo, ahora, la responsabilidad del desarrollo de tu fe ha cambiado. La decisión de recibir el sacramento de la Confirmación es tuya. La aceptación del sacramento de la Confirmación es una proclamación personal y pública, por la cual tú eliges seguir las huellas de Jesucristo. Este es el momento en tu vida espiritual donde tú decides vivir la misión de Cristo y participar más activamente en la vida de la Iglesia.

En las diez lecciones pasadas se examinó el sacramento de la Confirmación. Revisemos las ideas y los elementos que has explorado durante de este periodo de preparación.

EL CRECIMIENTO ESPIRITUAL ES UN VIAJE DE TODA LA VIDA

Tú estás recorriendo un camino espiritual que inició con tu Bautismo y se dirige hacia la integridad y unión con Dios. Sin embargo, no se trata de un viaje fácil. Este es un viaje que pasa por tiempos difíciles y momentos de desafío. No perderás la esperanza en los tiempos adversos, porque eres consciente de los grandes aliados que tienes para ayudarte en el seguimiento de Jesús; en especial la comunidad de fe, la ayuda de Nuestro Señor mismo y los sacramentos de la Iglesia. No notarás un cambio drástico después de tu Confirmación. Sin embargo, por medio de la gracia de Dios, del poder del Espíritu Santo y por medio de tu propio compromiso, **serás confirmado en tu fe**. Recuerda siempre que una fe cristiana madura requiere un viaje de toda la vida.

LOS SACRAMENTOS DE INICIACIÓN

Los cristianos son incorporados en Cristo por medio de los sacramentos de iniciación: el Bautismo, la Confirmación y la Eucaristía.

En la Iglesia primitiva, cuando una persona deseaba participar de modo pleno dentro de la comunidad cristiana, él o ella tenían que recorrer un periodo relativamente largo de estudio y preparación llamado catecumenado. Después de este periodo de preparación, el catecúmeno recibía el Bautismo, la Confirmación y la Eucaristía. Todo esto en una única y magnífica celebración que tenía lugar durante la Pascua.

Hoy en día, la Confirmación también resalta el sí personal del creyente a Jesús por medio del compromiso genuino de involucrarse en la vida de la Iglesia.

HISTORIA DEL SACRAMENTO DE LA CONFIRMACIÓN

El sacramento de la Confirmación ha cambiado a través de los siglos, e incluso ahora, se está haciendo un esfuerzo por definir de modo más claro **su significado y propósito**. Tú ya has estudiado algunos de estos cambios. Has descubierto que originalmente los sacramentos de iniciación, el Bautismo, la Confirmación y la Eucaristía, se celebraban en la Vigilia Pascual después de un largo periodo de preparación. Para aquellos que entran a formar parte de la Iglesia y nunca han sido bautizados, los tres sacramentos se celebran todavía en este orden durante la Vigilia Pascual. Hubo momentos en los que estos sacramentos estuvieron separados. Cuando se bautizaba a un bebé de padres cristianos, correspondía a los papás la responsabilidad de transmitir la fe de la comunidad a los niños. El sacramento de la Confirmación también asumió una nueva dimensión. **Los recién confirmados reciben una mayor responsabilidad en el desarrollo de su fe.**

Cuando recibes la Confirmación, se espera de ti una mayor contribución por parte tuya en favor del trabajo de la Iglesia, de la misión que Cristo mismo realizó. Esa participación en la vida de la Iglesia requiere una decisión bien pensada y, por lo tanto, muchos obispos piden que la persona que va a ser confirmada sea lo suficientemente madura para tomar esta decisión. Por ello en muchas diócesis se confirma a los cristianos durante su adolescencia.

"BE SEALED WITH THE GIFT OF THE HOLY SPIRIT"

The sacrament of confirmation is the celebration of your "anointing," your commissioning by the Holy Spirit to love as Jesus loved. You are "sealed with the Gift of the Holy Spirit."

This Spirit expresses itself differently through different people, yet each anointed Christian is sealed with the same Spirit that anointed Jesus in his ministry. The Spirit strengthens and empowers each of you with the gifts of wisdom, understanding, right judgment, courage, knowledge, reverence, and wonder in God's presence—attributes that characterized Jesus' life.

Because you have the "breath of life"—God's life is within you—and because you will be commissioned with the gifts of the Spirit in confirmation, your daily lives have the opportunity to blossom and bring forth fruit—the fruit of the Spirit. The fruits of the Spirit include joy, faith, charity, patience, kindness, peace, generosity, gentleness, modesty, goodness, self-control, and chastity.

CHRISTIANS AS WOMEN AND MEN OF SERVICE

Confirmation is the "active" part of the initiation process. It is a sacrament that asks you not only to believe in Jesus Christ, but also to live his life daily. Living the life of Jesus means living a life of service, and service means responding to others' needs—in your home, in your Church community, in your city or town, in your nation, and even in your world. This commitment to concern for others is an essential part of the sacrament of confirmation.

THE RITE OF CONFIRMATION

The ritual of the sacrament is filled with signs of the presence of love, the presence of Christ. You explored the basic symbols around which the celebration ritual revolves: The Christian community assembled together; the bishop; the Word of God; the prayers; the laying on of hands; the anointing with oil; the Eucharist; the sponsors; and you. **All these important signs and symbols help us to effectively celebrate the solemn ritual** of this sacrament.

LA CONFIRMACIÓN para adolescentes

CONFIRMATION for teens

CONFIRMATION CANDIDATE

Retreat Day

Note to Leaders

This is designed as a group retreat, but it can be adapted by individuals unable to participate in the group retreat. If the group includes any who have not been part of your parish's confirmation preparation program, leaders should **provide name tags** and plan an activity that will introduce new members to the group.

Each participant will need a Bible, a notebook to be used as a "spiritual journal," and a pen. This retreat will require about five hours, including a break for lunch. The times listed are only guidelines—the lengths of various activities may be varied to meet the needs of the group. If time permits, **it would be ideal to celebrate the Eucharist** at the end of the retreat.

Because quiet reflection and journal writing are important components of this retreat, an atmosphere conducive to these activities will be most helpful. Weather permitting, the periods of time set aside for reflection and discernment would preferably take place outdoors **where the "rebirth" of nature might inspire "spiritual rebirth"** in the lives of the participants.

PARA LA CONFIRMACIÓN DE LOS CANDIDATOS

Día de retiro

Notas para los líderes del retiro

Este retiro está diseñado para hacerse en grupo, pero se puede adaptar para que puedan hacerlo individualmente aquellos que no puedan participar en el retiro de la parroquia. Si en el grupo hay quienes no han participado en el programa de preparación para la Confirmación de la parroquia, los líderes deben **proveer algunos gafetes** y organizar una actividad para introducir a esos nuevos miembros al grupo.

Cada participante va a necesitar una Biblia, una libreta (se usará como diario espiritual) y una lapicero. Este retiro tiene una duración de cinco horas, incluido el tiempo libre y la comida. La duración de cada una de las actividades puede variar de acuerdo con las necesidades del grupo. Si el tiempo lo permite, **sería muy bueno celebrar la Eucaristía** al finalizar el retiro.

Dado que reflexionar tranquilamente y escribir en los diarios es un elemento importante del retiro, se debe proveer una atmósfera propicia para realizar estas actividades. Si el clima lo permite, los periodos dedicados a la reflexión personal y al discernimiento se pueden llevar a cabo preferentemente al aire libre, **donde la naturaleza pueda inspirar** el crecimiento espiritual de los participantes.

DEBBIE REPP

THE RETREAT INTRODUCTION

8:30 a.m.

By this time, you have spent many hours learning about the sacrament of confirmation. You have learned that this sacrament will not magically transform you into a "better" Christian. Rather, through the power of the Holy Spirit and your own renewed commitment to your faith, confirmation marks a time when you choose to become more fully immersed in the life of your Church. Your faith journey now takes a quantum leap forward because the responsibility for your further faith development shifts from your parents and guardians—to YOU.

More than anything, the purpose of this retreat is to provide you with time—time for some serious reflection, discernment, and decision-making. This is the time to ask yourself the following questions:

1. To the best of my ability, am I spiritually prepared to receive the sacrament of confirmation?

2. If so, in what specific ways can I involve myself in the life of my Church that best suit my personality, interests, and God-given talents?

Remember, God made you the wonderful person you are. You are not expected to be "perfect." You are striving toward a deeper and more mature faith, but real Christian maturity is a journey that requires a lifetime. In other words, do not feel discouraged because you "don't have all the answers." The first part of this retreat focuses on who you are, right now, today. The second part attempts to help you find ways to serve your Church based on who you are.

SESSION ONE

8:40 a.m.

The entire group should gather in a place conducive to prayer, preferably outdoors. Each participant should have a Bible and a notebook with a pen.

Opening Prayer: Lord, open our hearts and our minds to your presence as we continue our preparation for the sacrament of confirmation. We gather here today for quiet time, for reflection, for prayer, and for self-discovery. Teach us to see ourselves through your loving and all-knowing eyes, so that we might better know ourselves and become more aware of the goodness inherent in each of us. Amen

Reading from Scripture: Luke 2:41-52 may be read aloud by one or two of the participants.

> *He said to them, "Why were you searching for me? Did you not know that I must be in my Father's house?" But they did not understand what he said to them. Luke 2:49-50*

Sung Prayer: A song or hymn that asks God for guidance and knowledge may be sung by the participants and leaders. If instrumentalists are unavailable to accompany the singing, a recording may be used. Song suggestions include:

- *Shepherd Me,* O God, Marty Haugen, G.I.A. Publications, Inc.
- *I Lift Up My Soul,* Tim Manion, NewDawn Music

DISCUSSION REFLECTION

9:00 a.m.

Group: In this reading, we realize that Jesus, too, was at one time an "adolescent." Like all of us, he had to discover who he was. Talk about the reading—in what ways can you relate to the young Jesus who was struggling for independence and self-realization? Can you understand the feelings and concerns of Mary and Joseph when they finally found their son?

Adolescence is a time of great self-discovery. It is a most important time in every person's life because self-knowledge is essential if one is to make lasting commitments and solid decisions. Before one can decide how he or she wants to give to the Church, one must know what he or she has to offer.

Individually: In the next 30 to 45 minutes, take a long walk outdoors. Try not to talk with others. Reflect on the natural world and study the details and subtleties of nature.

INTRODUCCIÓN AL RETIRO

8:30 a.m.

A esta altura, ya has dedicado tiempo suficiente al aprendizaje acerca del sacramento de la Confirmación. Has aprendido que este sacramento no te transformará por arte de magia en un mejor cristiano. Antes bien, por medio del poder del Espíritu Santo y tu compromiso de fe renovada, la Confirmación marca el inicio donde tú eliges involucrarte más en la vida de la Iglesia. Tu viaje de la fe da un paso adelante, dado que la responsabilidad para el desarrollo de tu fe pasa de tus padres o tutores a ti.

Antes que nada, el fin de este retiro es proporcionarte tiempo, tiempo para reflexionar seriamente, para discernir y para tomar decisiones. Este es el tiempo de hacerte las siguientes preguntas:

1. Siendo completamente honesto, ¿estoy preparado espiritualmente para recibir el sacramento de la Confirmación?

2. De ser así, ¿de qué modo puedo involucrarme en la vida de la Iglesia, logrando al mismo tiempo, que esto vaya de acuerdo con mi personalidad, mis intereses y con los dones que he recibido de Dios?

Recuerda que Dios te ha hecho la persona maravillosa que eres. No se espera de ti que seas perfecto. Tú estás luchando por alcanzar una fe más madura y profunda, pero la verdadera madurez cristiana es un viaje que requiere toda una vida. En otras palabras, no te sientas desanimado porque no tienes todas las respuestas a tus interrogantes. La primera parte de este retiro se centra en quién eres en este preciso momento. La segunda parte trata de ayudarte a encontrar el camino para servir a la Iglesia, basándose en lo que tú eres.

PRIMERA PARTE

8:40 a.m.

Todo el grupo debe reunirse en un lugar que sea propicio para la oración, de preferencia al aire libre. Cada participante debe tener la Biblia y una libreta con su pluma.

Oración inicial: Señor, al continuar con nuestra preparación para recibir el sacramento de la Confirmación, abre nuestros corazones y nuestras mentes a tu presencia. Nos reunimos el día de hoy aquí para tener un tiempo de tranquilidad, para reflexionar, para orar y para conocernos a nosotros mismos. Enséñanos a vernos a nosotros mismos a través de tus ojos amorosos y que todo lo saben, a fin de poder conocernos y así poder llegar a ser más conscientes de la profunda bondad que poseemos. Amén.

Lectura de la Escritura: el pasaje de Lc 2:41-52 puede leerse en voz alta por parte de uno o dos de los participantes.

> *Él les contestó: "¿Y por qué me buscaban? ¿No saben que yo debo estar donde mi Padre?" Pero ellos no comprendieron esta respuesta (Lc 2:49-50).*

Oración cantada: Tanto los líderes del retiro como los participantes, deben entonar un canto o himno en el que se pida luz y discernimiento a Dios. Si no hay instrumentos disponibles para acompañar el canto, se puede utilizar una grabación. Se sugiere:

- *Shepherd Me,* O God, Marty Haugen, G.I.A. Publications, Inc.
- *I Lift Up My Soul,* Tim Manion, New Dawn Music.
- *El Señor es mi luz y mi salvación* (Flor y canto 725)
- *Gusten y vean qué bueno es el Señor* (Flor y canto 177)

DISCUSIÓN Y REFLEXIÓN

9:00 a.m.

Grupo: En esta lectura nos damos cuenta de que Jesús también fue adolescente. Como todos nosotros, Él también tuvo que descubrir quién era. Comenta acerca de la lectura. ¿En qué modo te puedes relacionar con Jesús joven, quien luchaba también por su independencia y realización personal?

¿Entiendes los sentimientos y la preocupación de José y María cuando finalmente encontraron a su Hijo?

La adolescencia es un tiempo de grandes descubrimientos sobre uno mismo. Es una de las etapas más importantes en la vida de una persona, dado que el conocimiento de uno mismo es esencial si uno quiere tomar decisiones y compromisos duraderos. Antes de decidir lo que uno quiere darle a la Iglesia, es indispensable saber lo que uno tiene para ofrecer.

Individualmente: En los siguientes 30 o 45 minutos, da un paseo al aire libre. Trata de no hablar con los demás. Reflexiona acerca de la naturaleza y estudia sus detalles y sutilezas.

Think about what you can learn from nature. (If you cannot be outdoors, find a quiet, comfortable place and use your imagination to "walk" outdoors. Try to imagine being in the mountains, by the sea, or in a spring garden.) Reflect on the following questions. During your "journaling" time, you will be asked to record your answers. Be assured that your "spiritual journal" will remain completely confidential unless you choose to share it.

1 Did you see signs of "rebirth" and "reawakening" in the natural world? How can you relate the change from winter to spring to your own life?

2 Can the sacrament of confirmation be a chance for "rebirth" in your own life? How?

3 Reflect on who you are right now. What are your strengths? What are your shortcomings? What do you like to do in your spare time? What do you do that gives you a sense of self-fulfillment? When do you feel happiest? When do you feel down or confused? Who are your favorite people? Who are your heroes?

JOURNALING

9:45 a.m.

Your notebooks are to become your "spiritual journals"—written records of your innermost thoughts, feelings, struggles, and joys. A spiritual journal is an excellent tool for helping one "figure out" one's life, one small piece at a time. Hopefully, many of you already keep personal journals or diaries and feel comfortable writing down your thoughts and feelings. A spiritual journal simply adds the spiritual dimension or perspective. Spend the next 30 minutes "journaling." Record your observations about the natural world. Then record your responses to the three questions asked earlier. Attempt to be very honest. You do not have to write in complete sentences—sometimes simple phrases say all that needs to be said. Remember, your journals are private—they are tools for self-discovery that hopefully you will use for a lifetime!

BREAK

10:15 a.m.

SESSION TWO

10:30 a.m.

The entire group should again gather in a place conducive to prayer, preferably outdoors. Each participant should once again have a Bible and his or her "spiritual journal."

Gathering Prayer: Lord, continue to open our eyes, hearts, and minds as we seek to discover who we are. Help us to remember that we are your precious children and that you made us in your own image and likeness. Teach us to recognize and acknowledge the special talents and gifts you have bestowed on each of us. Teach us to respect the gifts and talents of others and to enjoy the unique personality of each member of our group. Help us not to fear being "different." Give us the courage to become young men and women who strive to build your kingdom here on earth. Amen

Reading from Scripture: John 13:1-17 may be read aloud by one or two participants.

> *"So if I, your Lord and Teacher, have washed your feet, you also ought to wash one another's feet. For I have set you an example, that you also should do as I have done to you." John 13:14-15*

Sung Prayer: Sing or listen to a song that celebrates our membership in the "Body of Christ." Song suggestions include:

- *Song of the Body of Christ*, David Haas, G.I.A. Publications, Inc.
- *One Bread, One Body*, John B. Foley, S.J., New Dawn Music

DISCUSSION | REFLECTION

10:45

Group: In this reading, we are not only taught how to serve one another, we are told we must serve one another if we are to be followers of Christ. Jesus makes it so clear: "You also should do." Discuss the many ways we can serve one another through our parish, school, or community. Describe the various ministries within the Church that are now or will soon become service options for you—for example, cantor, choir member, lector, hospitality minister, etc. Discuss possible service options available through your school—for example, tutor, library assistant, assistant coach, etc. Try to think of ways you can serve others in your neighborhood or community. Be realistic. Consider your age, availability of transportation, prior commitments, etc. Attempt to come up with several ways that young men and women can realistically and effectively serve one another and therefore become more involved in the life of the Church.

Individually: Again take time to walk alone outside. Take time to relax and to meditate on all you have discussed during the first two sessions. In the first session, you attempted to describe yourself—your interests, talents, shortcomings, and so on. With your own interests and talents in mind, come up with one or two ways that you might effectively serve others. Think simply and realistically.

Piensa acerca de lo que puedes aprender de ella. En caso de que no puedas estar en la naturaleza, busca un lugar tranquilo, cómodo y usa tu imaginación para caminar al aire libre. Imagina que estás en las montañas, cerca del mar o en un jardín. Medita acerca de las siguientes preguntas. Durante el tiempo para escribir en tu diario, se te pedirá que respondas por escrito a las preguntas. Asegúrate de que tu diario espiritual **permanezca completamente confidencial**, a menos que decidas compartirlo.

1. ¿Ves algún signo de renacimiento o florecimiento en la naturaleza? ¿De qué modo puedes relacionar el cambio del invierno a la primavera con tu propia vida?
2. ¿Es posible que el sacramento de la Confirmación sea una oportunidad para el renacimiento de tu propia vida?, ¿de qué modo?
3. Reflexiona acerca de quién eres en este momento: ¿cuáles son tus fortalezas?, ¿cuáles son tus deficiencias?, ¿qué te gusta hacer durante tus tiempos libres? De todo lo que realizas, ¿qué es lo que te hace sentir realizado personalmente?, ¿cuándo te sientes más feliz?, ¿cuándo te sientes decaído o confundido?, ¿quiénes son tus personas favoritas?, ¿quiénes son tus héroes?

DIARIO ESPIRITUAL

9:45 a.m.

Tus libretas son tu diario espiritual, apunta en ellas tus pensamientos más íntimos, tus sentimientos, tus luchas y tus alegrías. Un diario espiritual es una gran herramienta que te sirve para examinar tu vida momento a momento. Ojalá que la mayoría lleve ya un diario espiritual o simplemente un diario, y se sientan cómodos escribiendo sus pensamientos y sentimientos. Un diario espiritual añade simplemente una dimensión y perspectiva espiritual. Ocupa los siguientes 30 minutos para escribir en tu diario espiritual. Anota tus observaciones acerca de la naturaleza. Enseguida escribe las respuestas a las tres preguntas que se hicieron anteriormente. Trata de ser lo más honesto posible. **No tienes que escribir grandes discursos**, pues, algunas veces, frases simples expresan todo lo que hay que decir. Recuerda que tu diario es privado. Se trata de una herramienta para el conocimiento personal que es de esperarse que utilices toda la vida.

TIEMPO LIBRE

10:15 a.m.

SEGUNDA PARTE

10:30 a.m.

Todo el grupo debe reunirse una vez más en un lugar propicio para la oración y, de preferencia, al aire libre. Cada uno de los participantes debe traer consigo una Biblia junto con su diario espiritual.

Oración para la reunión: Señor, continúa abriendo nuestros ojos, nuestros corazones y nuestras mentes, mientras buscamos descubrir quiénes somos. Ayúdanos a recordar que nosotros somos hijos queridos y que Tú nos hiciste a imagen y semejanza tuya. Enséñanos a reconocer y a admitir los talentos y dones tan especiales que nos has otorgado a cada uno de nosotros. Enséñanos a respetar los dones y talentos de los demás y a disfrutar la personalidad única de cada uno de los miembros de nuestro grupo. Ayúdanos a no temer ser diferentes. Danos el coraje de llegar a ser hombres y mujeres que luchan por construir tu Reino aquí en la Tierra. Amén.

Lectura de la Escritura: Juan 13:1-17, puede ser leído por uno o dos de los participantes.

> *"Pues si yo, siendo el Señor y el Maestro, les he lavado los pies, también ustedes deben lavarse los pies unos a otros. Yo les he dado ejemplo y ustedes deben hacer como he hecho yo" (Jn 13:14-15).*

Oración cantada: Canten o escuchen una canción que celebre nuestra pertenencia al Cuerpo de Cristo. Las sugerencias son:

- *Song of the Body of Christ,* David Haas, G.I.A. Publications, Inc.
- *One bread, One Body,* John B. Foley, S.J., New Dawn Music
- *Un solo Señor* (Flor y canto 721)
- *Un pueblo que camina* (Flor y canto 686)

DISCUSIÓN Y REFLEXIÓN

10:45 a.m.

Grupo: en la lectura no solo se nos enseña cómo servirnos unos a otros, antes bien, se nos dice que tenemos que hacerlo si queremos ser seguidores de Cristo. Jesús es muy claro: "ustedes deben hacer". Discute acerca de todas las posibilidades que tenemos para servirnos unos a otros por medio de la parroquia, la escuela o la comunidad. Describe los diversos ministerios dentro de la Iglesia que son o serán pronto opciones de servicio para ti, por ejemplo: cantor, miembro del coro, lector, ministro hospitalario, etc. Discute las posibles opciones de servicio por medio de tu escuela, por ejemplo: tutor, asistente de biblioteca, asistente del entrenador, etc. Intenta pensar acerca de modos en los que puedes servir a los demás en tu colonia o en tu comunidad. Sé realista. Considera

Do not think too big and risk overwhelming yourself. If you are a shy person, consider working with an individual or a very small group, perhaps young children. If you are comfortable being in front of larger groups of people, consider developing your skills as a lector, church musician, or choir member. However you choose to live your faith, make sure you feel comfortable doing what you do. Serving others can, and should, be a positive and joyful experience!

JOURNALING

11:30 a.m.

As in Session 1, spend the next half hour recording your thoughts regarding the ideas discussed in the Discussion/Reflection part of this session. Remember that your journal is a tool for self-discovery. Be free with your ideas.

LUNCH

12:00 p.m.

SESSION THREE

12:45 p.m.

Following the lunch break, the participants and leaders again gather in a place suitable for prayer. Each person should have a Bible and a pen. This handout will be used for the written work in this final session. (Extra loose-leaf paper should be available to participants.)

Gathering Prayer: Lord, we have spent the last few hours looking within ourselves. We have attempted to recognize our unique talents and gifts—and we have searched for ways that will allow us to share these gifts in the service of others. After doing our very best to "know" ourselves, we now ask your help once again. We ask you to assist us in preparing our hearts and minds for the reception of the sacrament of confirmation. Help us to feel comfortable and positive about your offer of grace through this sacrament. May your Holy Spirit descend upon us and fill us with burning desire to become actively involved in the work of your Church and in the building up of your kingdom here on this earth. Amen

Reading from Scripture: 1 Corinthians 12:1-31. This is a lengthy passage which should be read aloud by two or three readers.

> *To each is given the manifestation of the Spirit for the common good.*
> *1 Corinthians 12:7*

Sung Prayer: A song which celebrates the power of the Holy Spirit should be sung or listened to at this time. Song suggestions include:

- *Send Us Your Spirit*, David Haas, G.I.A. Publications, Inc.
- *Spirit, Come*, Gregory Norbet, OCP Publications
- *Eye Has Not Seen*, Marty Haugen, G.I.A. Publications, Inc.

CONCLUDING ACTIVITY

1:00 p.m.

Use the next several minutes to thoughtfully answer the following questions. There are no "right" or "wrong" answers. Write your answers on a separate sheet of paper. If you are comfortable sharing your responses with others, the papers may be "offered" during the Preparation of the Gifts at a eucharistic liturgy connected with this retreat. If you prefer to keep your responses confidential, feel free to do so.

1. **Do you feel you have an adequate understanding** of the sacrament of confirmation? If you have questions that are still unanswered, please write them down so that they can be addressed in future discussions.

2. **At this point in your preparation for the sacrament of confirmation,** do you feel you have the spiritual foundation necessary to receive the sacrament? If you have serious doubts about your faith or your spiritual preparedness, do not hesitate to confide in someone who can help you. Your retreat leaders can guide you to a priest or catechist who can help you sort things out. (But don't forget—EVERYONE experiences doubt at one time or another. Mature Christian faith takes most of us a lifetime to develop—and even then, we will not be perfect, and we will still experience doubts now and then.)

3. **During this retreat, you have spent time** taking a serious look at yourself. You have done your best to honestly assess your own strengths and weaknesses, your likes and dislikes, and your special talents or gifts. With this knowledge in mind, how could you best serve your Church and become more fully immersed in its life? (These responses are by no means commitments—rather they are realistic possibilities and guidelines.)

When you have completed your responses, please sit quietly until everyone is finished.

Closing Prayer: At this time, the participants and leaders are encouraged to pray spontaneously—praising and thanking God for this day and asking the Holy Spirit for guidance and strength.

CLOSE

1:30 p.m.

tu edad, tu disponibilidad de transporte, compromisos ya adquiridos, etc. Trata de sugerir algunas formas realistas y efectivas de cómo un joven puede servir a los demás y, en consecuencia, involucrarse más en la vida de la Iglesia.

Individualmente: Una vez más, tómate tu tiempo para caminar afuera solo. Dedica tiempo para relajarte y para meditar en todo aquello que has discutido durante las primeras dos sesiones. En la primera parte, trataste de describirte a ti mismo, tus talentos, tus intereses y tus carencias. Con tus propios intereses y talentos en mente, piensa en una o dos formas de servir a los demás. Piensa de modo simple y realista. No pienses en grande, pues te arriesgas a abrumarte de trabajo. Si eres una persona tímida, es bueno que consideres trabajar con una sola persona o con grupos pequeños, quizá niños. Si te sientes bien estando con grupos grandes, piensa en desarrollar tus habilidades como lector, músico dentro de la iglesia o miembro del coro. Cuando escojas cómo vivir tu fe, asegúrate de sentirte cómodo con aquello que realizas. El servicio a los demás es y debería ser una experiencia positiva y alegre.

DIARIO ESPIRITUAL

11:30 a.m.

Como en la primera sesión, ocupa la siguiente media hora anotando tus pensamientos acerca de las ideas vistas en la parte de discusión y reflexión. Recuerda que el diario es una herramienta para el descubrimiento personal. Siéntete en libertad con tus ideas.

COMIDA

12:00 p.m.

TERCERA PARTE

12:45 p.m.

Después de la comida, los participantes y líderes del retiro pueden reunirse una vez más en un lugar apropiado para la oración. Cada persona debe tener una Biblia y un lapicero. Este folleto se empleará como material para escribir el trabajo de esta última sesión. Debe haber disponible algo de papel extra para todos los participantes.

Oración para la reunión: Señor, hemos empleado las últimas horas examinándonos a nosotros mismos. Hemos intentado reconocer nuestros talentos y dones únicos. Al mismo tiempo hemos intentado buscar caminos que nos permitan compartir estos dones para servir a los demás. Después de hacer nuestro mejor esfuerzo para conocernos a nosotros mismos, te pedimos tu ayuda una vez más. Te pedimos que nos asistas en la preparación de nuestros corazones y nuestras mentes para recibir el sacramento de la Confirmación. Ayúdanos a sentirnos cómodos y con espíritu positivo acerca del ofrecimiento que nos haces de tu gracia por medio de este sacramento. Que tu Espíritu Santo descienda sobre nosotros. Que nos llene con un ardiente deseo de ser miembros activos en la obra de tu Iglesia y en la edificación de tu Reino aquí en la Tierra. Amén.

Lectura de la Escritura: 1 Cor 12:1-31, se trata de un pasaje extenso que dos o más participantes deberán leer en voz alta.

> *"La manifestación del Espíritu que a cada uno se le da es para provecho común" 1 Cor 12:7.*

Oración cantada: En este momento debe entonarse una canción que celebre el poder del Espíritu Santo. Las canciones que se sugieren son estas:

- *Send Us Your Spirit,* David Haas, G.I.A. Publications, Inc.
- *Spirit, Come,* Gregory Norbet, OCP Publications
- *Eye Has Not Seen,* Marty Haugen, G.I.A. Publications, Inc.
- *Envía, Señor, tu Espíritu* (Flor y canto 380)
- *Envía tu Espíritu* (Flor y canto 217)

ACTIVIDAD CONCLUSIVA

1:00 p.m.

Usa los minutos siguientes para responder cuidadosamente a las siguientes preguntas. Aquí no existen respuestas correctas o incorrectas. Escribe tus respuestas en una hoja aparte. Si estás de acuerdo en compartir tus respuestas con los demás, puedes ofrecer las hojas durante la preparación de los dones en la Celebración Eucarística que se tendrá al final del retiro. Si prefieres mantener tus respuestas confidenciales, siéntete libre de hacerlo así.

1. **¿Sientes que tienes una comprensión adecuada** de lo que es el sacramento de la Confirmación? Si tienes todavía preguntas que necesitan alguna respuesta, escríbelas para que puedan ser atendidas después.
2. **A esta altura de tu preparación para el sacramento de la Confirmación,** ¿sientes que tienes los fundamentos suficientes para recibir el sacramento? Si tienes serias dudas acerca de tu fe y de tu disposición espiritual, que no te dé pena recurrir a alguien que pueda ayudarte. Los líderes del retiro pueden ponerte en contacto con un sacerdote o catequista que pueda ayudarte a resolver las cosas. Sin embargo, no olvides que todos experimentamos la duda en algún momento. A la mayoría nos toma toda una vida formar una fe cristiana madura e, incluso al lograrla, seguiremos aún sin ser perfectos. Todavía experimentaremos dudas de vez en cuando.
3. **Durante este retiro, has dedicado tiempo** para examinarte a ti mismo. Has hecho lo mejor de tu parte para evaluar tus propias fuerzas y debilidades, lo que te gusta y aquello que te disgusta, y también tus talentos y dones. Con este conocimiento en mente, ¿cómo podrías servir del mejor modo posible a la Iglesia y participar más en su vida? Estas respuestas no son, de ningún modo, compromisos. Son, más bien, posibilidades y directrices realistas.

Cuando hayas terminado tus respuestas, permanece en silencio hasta que todos hayan terminado.

Oración final: En este momento se pide que los participantes y líderes del retiro hagan una oración espontánea, en la que adoren y den gracias a Dios por este día, y pidan al Espíritu Santo que sea su guía y fortaleza.

FINAL

1:30 p.m.

Basado en el texto original escrito por Michael Ketterhagen. Un agradecimiento especial a los padres Paul Niemann y Joe Kempf. Editado por Marco Batta. Diseño de Maggie Bubenik. ©2013 Libros Liguori, Liguori, MO 63057-9999.

Publicado con aprobación eclesiástica. Textos tomados del *Ritual para la Confirmación*, Editorial Buena Prensa 1999. Impreso en Estados Unidos.

Las citas de la Escritura están tomadas de la *Biblia Latinoamérica*, disponible en www.sobicain.org. Usada con permiso. Todos los derechos reservados.

Based on the original by Michael Ketterhagen. Special thanks to Rev. Paul Niemann and Rev. Joe Kempf. Edited by Lauren K. Borstell. Design by Maggie Bubenik.

©2013 Liguori Publications, Liguori, MO 63057-9999.

Published with ecclesiastical approval. Compliant with *The Roman Missal*, third edition. Printed in U.S.A.

Scripture quotation is taken from the *New Revised Standard Version Bible*, © 1989, Division of Christian Education of the National Council of Churches of Christ in the United States of America. Reprinted with permission. All rights reserved.

"RECIBE POR ESTA SEÑAL EL DON DEL ESPÍRITU SANTO"

El sacramento de la Confirmación es la celebración de tu unción, de la misión que el Espíritu Santo te da de amar como Jesús amó. Tú eres marcado con el don del Espíritu Santo.

El Espíritu se expresa de diversas maneras y por medio de diversas personas. Sin embargo, cada cristiano es marcado con el mismo Espíritu que ungió a Jesús para su ministerio. El Espíritu fortalece y robustece a cada uno con el don de sabiduría, inteligencia, fortaleza, ciencia, piedad y temor de Dios; atributos que también caracterizaron la vida de Jesús.

Dado que ustedes poseen el aliento de vida, que es la vida divina dentro de ustedes y porque ustedes recibirán los dones del Espíritu en la Confirmación, su vida diaria tiene oportunidad de florecer y dar frutos, los frutos del Espíritu Santo que son: amor, alegría, paz, paciencia, longanimidad, bondad, benignidad, mansedumbre, fe, modestia, continencia y castidad.

LOS CRISTIANOS, HOMBRES Y MUJERES DE SERVICIO

La Confirmación es la parte activa del proceso de iniciación. Este es un sacramento que no solo te pide creer en Jesucristo, sino que también te pide vivir su vida día a día. Vivir la vida de Jesús significa vivir una vida de servicio. El servicio significa, a su vez, dar una respuesta a las necesidades de los demás: en tu propia casa, en tu comunidad parroquial, en tu propia ciudad o población, en tu país e incluso en el mundo. Este compromiso de preocuparte por los demás es una parte esencial del sacramento de la Confirmación.

EL RITO DE LA CONFIRMACIÓN

El ritual del sacramento está repleto de signos de la presencia del amor, de la presencia de Cristo. Tú ya estudiaste los símbolos básicos que rodean el desarrollo del rito de la celebración: la comunidad cristiana reunida, el obispo, la Palabra de Dios, las oraciones, la imposición de las manos, la unción con el óleo, la Eucaristía, los padrinos y tú. Todos estos signos y símbolos importantes **nos ayudan a celebrar eficazmente el rito** solemne de este sacramento.

ACTIVITY JUST FOR YOU

LETTER TO THE BISHOP

Once you feel that you really understand the sacrament of confirmation, and once you have decided that you wish to accept this great gift from God, it is time to express this decision by asking to be confirmed. Each of you should write a personal letter to your bishop, requesting that you be confirmed. **The letter should clearly express** the facts **(1)** that receiving the sacrament of confirmation is your decision; **(2)** that you have prepared for the sacrament through study, instruction, and prayer; and **(3)** that you have already accepted the responsibility of living a more mature Christian life by being of service to the community.

Here is one example of what you might say to the bishop in your letter. Do not follow this example strictly, but do try to include the three points mentioned above. Write to the bishop with seriousness and respect—but also write **"from your heart."**

EXAMPLE

Dear Bishop N.,

I have been preparing for the celebration of the sacrament of confirmation for quite some time, and I would like to be confirmed in my faith. I would like to be "sealed with the Gift of the Holy Spirit."

As a teenager, I realize that more and more maturity will be expected from me. This is true of my faithlife also. I would like to be strengthened by the gift of the Holy Spirit as I continue on my journey of faith.

To prepare for this sacrament, I have faithfully attended the catechetical instructions at my parish, and tried to be of service to others by (list here the specific ways you have been of service to others). In the future, I intend to continue serving my community by (list ways you intend to continue being of service after you have been confirmed).

As you can see, I have chosen to be part of the mission of Christ. I am now formally requesting the sacrament of confirmation.

Thank you very much.

Gratefully,

(your full name)

Confirmation candidate of ______________________________ Parish

TAREA SOLO PARA TI

CARTA AL OBISPO

Una vez que hayas entendido lo que es el sacramento de la Confirmación y una vez que hayas tomado la decisión de acoger este don de Dios, es tiempo de expresar esta decisión pidiendo ser confirmado. Cada uno de ustedes debe escribir una carta personal a su obispo, en la cual piden ser confirmados. La carta **debe expresar** claramente los siguientes puntos: **(1)** recibir el sacramento de la Confirmación es decisión tuya; **(2)** te has preparado para recibir el sacramento por medio del estudio, de la instrucción y de la oración; **(3)** has aceptado la responsabilidad de vivir una vida cristiana más madura por medio del servicio a la comunidad.

Aquí se expone un ejemplo de lo que debería decir la carta al obispo. No es necesario que sigas al pie de la letra este ejemplo, pero no se deben omitir los tres puntos mencionados anteriormente. Escribe al obispo con seriedad y respeto, pero también **desde el corazón**.

ESTIMADO

Obispo N.,

Durante este tiempo, me he estado preparando para la celebración del sacramento de la Confirmación y quisiera ser confirmado en mi fe. Quiero ser marcado "con el don del Espíritu Santo".

Como adolescente me doy cuenta de que se me va a exigir una mayor madurez. Sé que lo mismo se me va a pedir acerca de mi fe. Quiero ser fortalecido con el don del Espíritu Santo mientras continúo mi viaje en la fe.

Como preparación para este sacramento he asistido sin falta a las clases de catecismo impartidas en mi parroquia. He tratado de servir a los demás por medio de (haz una breve lista de los servicios que has prestado a los demás). En un futuro, tengo la intención de continuar con mi servicio a la comunidad por medio de (haz una lista de aquellos servicios que tienes en mente realizar después de tu Confirmación).

Como podrá notar, he tomado la decisión de ser parte de la misión de Cristo y estoy pidiendo formalmente el sacramento de la Confirmación.

Muchas gracias.

Con gratitud,

(Nombre completo)

Candidato para la Confirmación de la parroquia:

_______________________________ (Nombre de la parroquia)

Basado en el texto original escrito por Michael Ketterhagen. Un agradecimiento especial a los padres Paul Niemann y Joe Kempf. Editado por Marco Batta. Diseño de Maggie Bubenik. ©2013 Libros Liguori, Liguori, MO 63057-9999.

Publicado con aprobación eclesiástica. Textos tomados del *Ritual para la Confirmación*, Editorial Buena Prensa 1999. Impreso en Estados Unidos.

LIBROS LIGUORI

Based on the original by Michael Ketterhagen. Special thanks to Rev. Paul Niemann and Rev. Joe Kempf. Edited by Lauren K. Borstell. Design by Maggie Bubenik.

©2013 Liguori Publications, Liguori, MO 63057-9999.

Published with ecclesiastical approval. Compliant with *The Roman Missal*, third edition. Printed in U.S.A.

EL SACRAMENTO DE LA CONFIRMACIÓN

En este momento, el sacramento de la Confirmación en cuanto tal es conferido a los candidatos. Ellos han preparado sus corazones para recibir el sello del Espíritu Santo. El obispo pide a la asamblea reunida que ore por los candidatos. Después de que todos hayan orado en silencio, el obispo extiende sus manos sobre los candidatos pidiendo al Espíritu Santo que venga con su poder sobre ellos. Con los brazos extendidos ora así:

> *Dios Todopoderoso, Padre de nuestro Señor Jesucristo, que regeneraste, por el agua y el Espíritu Santo, a estos siervos tuyos y los libraste del pecado: escucha nuestra oración y envía sobre ellos el Espíritu Santo Paráclito; llénalos de espíritu de sabiduría y de inteligencia, de espíritu de consejo y de fortaleza, de espíritu de ciencia y de piedad; y cólmalos del espíritu de tu santo temor. Por Jesucristo nuestro Señor. Amén.*
> *(Ritual de la Confirmación, 25).*

Enseguida le traen al obispo el crisma. **Cada uno de los candidatos es presentado al obispo**; el candidato se coloca de pie o de rodillas ante él. El padrino pone su mano sobre el hombro del candidato y el obispo con su dedo pulgar, humedecido en el santo crisma, hace el signo de la cruz en la frente del que va ser confirmado mientras dice:

"N., recibe por esta señal el don del Espíritu Santo".

A lo que responde el neoconfirmado: *"Amén".*

Después de lo cual, el obispo da una señal de paz a los neoconfirmados y **la comunidad parroquial les ofrece su apoyo** por medio del signo de la paz o por medio de una oración ofrecida como comunidad.

LA EUCARISTÍA

El mejor contexto para celebrar el sacramento de la Confirmación es el de la Liturgia Eucarística. Con la renovación de las promesas bautismales que preceden a la Confirmación y seguida de la Liturgia Eucarística, los tres sacramentos de iniciación forman una unidad.

ORACIÓN FINAL

Al final de la liturgia y antes de que todos se retiren en procesión ordenada, el obispo da una bendición solemne a la comunidad reunida. Esta bendición complementa el rito de la Confirmación:

> *Dios Padre todopoderoso, que los adoptó como hijos, haciéndolos renacer del agua y del Espíritu Santo, los bendiga y los haga siempre dignos de su amor.*
> **Amén**

El Hijo unigénito de Dios, que prometió que el Espíritu de verdad estaría siempre en la Iglesia, los bendiga y los fortalezca en la confesión de la fe verdadera.

Amén

El Espíritu Santo, que encendió en el corazón de los discípulos el fuego del amor, los bendiga y, congregándolos en la unidad, les conduzca a los gozos del Reino Eterno.

Amén

El obispo añade inmediatamente:

Y la bendición de Dios todopoderoso Padre, Hijo y Espíritu Santo descienda sobre ustedes.

Amén

ACTIVITY FOR THE FAMILY

There are some practical points to consider before receiving the sacrament of confirmation. Ultimately, these decisions are yours, but it might be helpful to talk about the following points with your parents or loved ones.

YOUR SPONSOR

First, let's spend some time clarifying the role of the sponsor. Your sponsor should be a person who can travel with you on your journey to Christian maturity. This person should really know you and be readily available to listen to your concerns and questions about your faith or about the Church. One of your godparents, who may already be very much involved in your life, would generally be the best choice for the role. An aunt or an uncle might be an appropriate choice if he or she lives within a reasonable distance. Another choice for a sponsor might be a teacher, catechist, or parishioner whom you admire, see quite often, and with whom you will likely have a **long-term relationship**.

Whomever you choose, your sponsor must be sufficiently mature, belong to the Catholic Church, and be initiated into the three sacraments of baptism, confirmation, and Eucharist. Most importantly, your sponsor and you should have more than an "acquaintance-type" relationship. Your sponsor needs to be a spiritual friend to you.

YOUR CONFIRMATION NAME

One of the traditional practices in the Church at the time of confirmation is choosing a name that will remind you of this sacrament. Your prayerful reflection will help you determine that name. You might want to recommit yourself to your baptismal name, especially after you reflect on its meaning and discover some of the people who shared your name in Christian history. **You might want to choose the name of a saint** who represents the type of Christian you wish to be. Whether you decide to stay with your baptismal name or pick a new name, take the time to research and explore the root meaning of the name, for as Scripture says, God calls each of us by name (see Isaiah 43:1).

READINESS FOR THE SACRAMENT

The most important of these practical concerns is your personal "readiness" for the sacrament. Confirmation involves no "magic." If you truly wish to become "fully immersed in the life of your Church," you will need to honor your commitment through real work and effort. Ask yourself the questions: "Am I ready to commit myself to Christ's mission? Am I really ready to be confirmed?" Readiness is not determined by parents, teachers, or pastors. Readiness is not determined by age or grade level. Your friends' readiness does not determine your own readiness.

Readiness to say, "Yes, I want to commit myself to Christ and live a full and involved Christian life" **requires a very mature, honest decision**. If, after prayerful reflection and consultation with your parents and your pastor, you choose to postpone your decision to be confirmed, you again are making a mature, honest decision, and it will be respected.

Remember, however, you do not have to be a "saint" to be ready for confirmation. You do not have to be "perfect" or "have it all together." Faith is a great journey—you must only be willing to grow and to travel in the footsteps of Jesus.

TAREA EN FAMILIA

Hay algunos puntos prácticos que tienes que considerar antes de recibir el sacramento de la Confirmación. Aunque, en última instancia, estas decisiones las tomas tú, sería de gran ayuda que hablaras de ello con tus padres o seres queridos.

TU PADRINO

Primero dediquemos un tiempo para aclarar el papel del padrino. Tu padrino debe ser una persona que camine junto a ti en tu viaje hacia la madurez cristiana. Esta persona debe conocerte y estar disponible para escuchar tus preocupaciones y preguntas acerca de tu fe y de la Iglesia. Uno de los que ya fueron padrinos de Bautismo y que ha estado involucrado en tu vida, sería el indicado para cumplir este papel. Un tío o tía sería también una opción apropiada, siempre y cuando viva cerca. Otra de las opciones podría ser un profesor, un catequista o un parroquiano a quien tú admires mucho, que veas seguido y con quien podrías tener **una relación duradera**.

Quien quiera que escojas, debe ser un padrino suficientemente maduro, que sea parte de la Iglesia Católica y que haya recibido los sacramentos del Bautismo, la Confirmación y la Eucaristía. Y lo que es más importante, tu padrino y tú deben ser entre sí algo más que simples conocidos. Tu padrino debe ser tu amigo espiritual.

TU NOMBRE DE CONFIRMACIÓN

Una de las prácticas tradicionales de la Iglesia en el momento de la Confirmación, es la de escoger un nombre que te hará recordar este sacramento. Tu reflexión en la oración te ayudará a escoger este nombre. Querrás quizá comprometerte de nuevo con tu nombre de Bautismo, en especial si has reflexionado acerca de su significado y has descubierto algunas personas que han compartido el mismo nombre a lo largo de la historia cristiana. **Quizá quieras escoger el nombre de algún santo** que representa el tipo de cristiano que tú quieres ser. De cualquier modo, si decides quedarte con tu nombre o elegir otro, toma tu tiempo para reflexionar en sus orígenes y su significado, pues la Escritura dice: "Yavé llama a cada uno por su nombre".

DISPONIBILIDAD PARA EL SACRAMENTO

La más importante de todas estas preocupaciones es tu disponibilidad personal para recibir el sacramento. La Confirmación no es algo mágico. Si deseas realmente lograr sumergirte en la vida de la Iglesia, necesitarás hacer honor a tu compromiso a través del trabajo y el esfuerzo. Hazte estas preguntas: ¿Estoy listo para comprometerme con la misión de Cristo? ¿Estoy listo para recibir la Confirmación? La disponibilidad no depende de los padres de familia, de los maestros o de los sacerdotes. La disponibilidad no se determina por la edad o el grado escolar. La disponibilidad de tus amigos no determina la tuya.

La disponibilidad para decir "sí, yo quiero comprometerme con Cristo y vivir una vida cristiana plena y comprometida", requiere **una decisión madura y honesta**. Si después de reflexionar en la oración y habiéndolo consultado con tus padres y el sacerdote, decides posponer tu decisión para ser confirmado, estás haciendo una decisión madura, honesta; y esta será respetada.

De cualquier modo recuerda que no se necesita ser un santo para estar listo para la Confirmación. No tienes que ser perfecto o tenerlo todo arreglado. La fe es un gran viaje, solo tienes que estar dispuesto a hacerla crecer y estar decidido a recorrer las huellas de Jesús.

Basado en el texto original escrito por Michael Ketterhagen. Un agradecimiento especial a los padres Paul Niemann y Joe Kempf. Editado por Marco Batta. Diseño de Maggie Bubenik.

Publicado con aprobación eclesiástica. Textos tomados del *Ritual para la Confirmación*, Editorial Buena Prensa 1999. Impreso en Estados Unidos.

LIBROS LIGUORI

Based on the original by Michael Ketterhagen. Special thanks to Rev. Paul Niemann and Rev. Joe Kempf. Edited by Lauren K. Borstell. Design by Maggie Bubenik.

Published with ecclesiastical approval. Compliant with *The Roman Missal*, third edition. Printed in U.S.A.

LA ASAMBLEA DE LA COMUNIDAD CRISTIANA

Cuando la comunidad se reúne en la fe, la asamblea es la Iglesia de Jesucristo. Cuando este grupo de creyentes está reunido, ellos hacen presentes las enseñanzas y la vida del Señor. En especial, su promesa de permanecer presente cuando uno o más estuvieran reunidos en su nombre. La comunidad es el Reino de Dios en la tierra. El reto de este sacramento es que la comunidad dé continuidad al Reino y que lo expanda tanto en la Tierra, como en el Cielo.

Los sacramentos son expresiones de la fe de la comunidad. En la comunidad el Espíritu viene y con los dones otorgados por Él, la comunidad es testigo y comparte la misión de Jesús con todo el mundo. La Confirmación es una celebración que renueva y aviva a toda la comunidad cristiana.

EL OBISPO

El obispo es el líder espiritual de la Iglesia local y es el eslabón que la une con la Iglesia universal. Él simboliza la unidad entre la comunidad parroquial y la Iglesia universal. Junto con los sacerdotes y diáconos, el obispo atiende a la comunidad diocesana y cada una de las parroquias en esa comunidad. Él tiene la responsabilidad primaria de asegurar que la vida del Espíritu se celebre adecuadamente. También, tiene la responsabilidad primaria de discernir los dones del Espíritu, así como se desarrollan en la vida local de la Iglesia. Junto a los otros obispos, representa a los Apóstoles en su papel de continuadores de la Iglesia de Jesucristo.

LOS CANDIDATOS PARA LA CONFIRMACIÓN

Ustedes también, como candidatos para recibir la Confirmación, son un signo. Son un signo del don del Espíritu Santo que se despliega en sus propias vidas, un signo de esperanza y renovación para la comunidad cristiana entera. Ustedes están celebrando un momento especial en el proceso de crecimiento hacia una vida plenamente cristiana, una vida que será una manifestación única y actual de la vida del Espíritu.

LOS PADRINOS

Los padrinos son un símbolo y son los representantes de la comunidad cristiana adulta. Tu padrino debería ser el mismo que te llevó a bautizar, de modo que se enfatice la unión entre el sacramento del Bautismo y el de la Confirmación. De no ser así, debes escoger a alguien que pueda acompañarte y asistirte en el desarrollo del don del Espíritu en tu vida; una persona que te ayudará a hacer madurar ese don dentro de la comunidad cristiana.

LA PALABRA DE DIOS

Las lecturas de la Escritura son un importante elemento dentro de la liturgia de la Confirmación, pues son un signo de la variedad del poder del Espíritu Santo que fluye a través de su Iglesia y a través de cada uno de los bautizados y confirmados. Y es por medio de esta palabra que la voluntad de Dios se manifiesta en la vida cristiana (cf. Rito de la Confirmación, 13).

La frase, "la Palabra de Dios", es en sí misma un símbolo verbal de la enseñanza, de la vida y del mensaje de Jesús. Por lo tanto, la lectura de la Escritura durante la celebración es la lectura de la misión de Cristo, la cual es sinónimo de fundamento de la fe de quienes, como tú, van a ser confirmados.

LA ORACIÓN DE LA COMUNIDAD

Cuando la comunidad cristiana, precedida por el obispo, ora por el don del Espíritu Santo, está significando su dependencia del Padre por medio del Hijo, para recibir el don del Espíritu. La comunidad, reunida contigo y dirigida por el obispo, reconoce su necesidad de permanecer abierta al Espíritu. A través de ese reconocimiento, se expresa la fe de la comunidad en la bondad del Padre que nos da todo lo que necesitamos para llevar a término la misión de Jesús.

LA IMPOSICIÓN DE LAS MANOS

La imposición de las manos es un gesto bíblico que guarda mucha importancia y, por el cual se le pide al Espíritu Santo que venga a ustedes. En el Evangelio Jesús cura a mucha gente solo con tocarla. Incluso narra la historia de la mujer con hemorragias que tocó su túnica, con la intención de ser curada, y que hizo que Jesús experimentara una fuerza saliendo de Él.

Hoy en día hay mucha información que nos indica que tocar es un acto significativo y que trae consigo la salud y la vida para la persona que es tocada. Tiene sentido que el poder del Espíritu Santo sea invocado por medio de la imposición de las manos y la oración, pidiendo el don del Espíritu para ustedes.

LA UNCIÓN CON EL CRISMA

El don del Espíritu se les confiere por medio de la imposición de las manos y la unción con el crisma sobre sus frentes mientras el obispo dice: "recibe por esta señal el don del Espíritu Santo". El crisma, un óleo que es bendecido por el obispo, es un signo del sacerdocio de Cristo al cual estamos todos llamados por medio de nuestro Bautismo.

LA EUCARISTÍA

Un contexto especialmente apropiado para la celebración de la Confirmación es la Liturgia Eucarística. La Eucaristía es el signo del modo de vida de Cristo. Por lo tanto, es un signo del camino a su muerte y resurrección. La Eucaristía significa la unidad de la Iglesia entera en Jesucristo y n os recuerda nuestra misión de trabajar por el Reino.

Estos signos y símbolos nos desafían constantemente a vivir nuestra vida cristiana en plenitud.

ACTIVITY FOR THE FAMILY

Every family, no matter how large or small, has meaningful traditions. These traditions, which often include powerful symbols, help to make birthdays, holidays, and vacations occasions which we eagerly anticipate. Family traditions and symbols **become precious memorie**s, and often we seek to continue the same traditions when we begin our own families.

Take a few moments to discuss traditions that are especially important to your family. **Do you have a special way of celebrating Christmas or Easter?** Talk about powerful symbols such as birthday cakes or Christmas trees. Imagine Christmas without a tree and all its glorious trimmings, or Advent without the Advent wreath. How does the absence of important symbols affect your celebration? Recall, too, your favorite family vacations. Is there a place you love to visit over and over?

Following a few minutes of brainstorming with your family or other loved ones, jot down a few sentences which describe an especially important family tradition. Include any signs or symbols that enhance the occasion or celebration. **Post this paper in a place where you will run across it** several times in the week ahead, and try to become more aware of the Church's traditions, signs, symbols, and liturgical colors, all of which enhance the assembly's celebration of the Sunday Eucharist.

FAVORITE FAMILY TRADITION

TAREA EN FAMILIA

Cada familia, sin importar si es grande o pequeña, tiene sus tradiciones llenas de significado. Estas tradiciones, que a menudo incluyen símbolos con gran contenido, nos ayudan a festejar los cumpleaños, los días festivos y las vacaciones, momentos todos estos que esperamos con tanta expectación. Las tradiciones familiares y los símbolos **se convierten en memorias imborrables**, y nosotros mismos buscamos continuar con esas tradiciones después de haber formado nuestras propias familias.

Tómate un momento para discutir las tradiciones que son especialmente importantes para tu familia. **¿Tienen algún modo especial de celebrar la Navidad o la Pascua?** Habla acerca de grandes símbolos como pasteles de cumpleaños o el árbol de Navidad. Imagina la Navidad sin el árbol y sin sus adornos, o el Adviento sin la corona. ¿Cómo la ausencia de símbolos importantes afecta su celebración? Recuerda también las vacaciones favoritas de la familia. ¿Hay algún lugar que te guste visitar una y otra vez?

Después de unos minutos de lluvia de ideas por parte de la familia o de algunos seres queridos, escribe algunas frases que describan una de las tradiciones más especiales para tu familia. Incluye algunos signos o símbolos que embellezcan la ocasión o la celebración. **Coloca esta hoja en un lugar donde puedas verla** constantemente durante la siguiente semana y trata al mismo tiempo de ser más consciente de las tradiciones, signos, símbolos y colores litúrgicos de la Iglesia, los cuales embellecen la asamblea de la Celebración Eucarística Dominical.

MI TRADICIÓN FAMILIAR FAVORITA

Basado en el texto original escrito por Michael Ketterhagen. Un agradecimiento especial a los padres Paul Niemann y Joe Kempf. Editado por Marco Batta. Diseño de Maggie Bubenik.

Publicado con aprobación eclesiástica. Textos tomados del *Ritual para la Confirmación*, Editorial Buena Prensa 1999. Impreso en Estados Unidos.

LIBROS LIGUORI™

Based on the original by Michael Ketterhagen. Special thanks to Rev. Paul Niemann and Rev. Joe Kempf. Edited by Lauren K. Borstell. Design by Maggie Bubenik.

Published with ecclesiastical approval. Compliant with *The Roman Missal*, third edition. Printed in U.S.A.

CONFIRMACIÓN Y ESTAR "DE SERVICIO"

Entonces, ¿qué significa ser partícipe de la misión de Jesús para un joven de hoy? Los Evangelios nos muestran continuamente que la misión de Jesús era una misión de servicio, **en especial a los pobres y marginados**.

Un verdadero servidor se olvida de sí mismo o de sí misma. Las necesidades de los demás son su prioridad. Como discípulos de Jesús, nuestro reto como servidores cristianos es el de ser cada vez más conscientes de las necesidades de aquellos que nos rodean y en especial de las personas que vemos a diario.

Aun así, no todos estamos llamados a ser misioneros en una tierra lejana. Algunas veces un aparente acto insignificante de delicadeza puede convertirse en un gran acto de servicio. Al momento de considerar posibles proyectos de servicio como preparación para la Confirmación, piensa primero en estos aspectos:

> **¿Qué clase de personalidad tengo?** ¿Eres acaso el tipo de organizador al que le gusta relacionarse con todo tipo de personas? ¿O quizá eres de esas personas a las que les gusta un trabajo personalizado y con grupos reducidos?
>
> **¿Qué es lo que te gusta hacer?** El servicio a los demás puede y debe ser algo que se disfruta y, a su vez, sea de provecho. Por ejemplo, si eres un experto en computación, ¿te gustaría dar tutoría a los estudiantes y donar tus talentos al servicio de la comunidad? Si amas el deporte, ¿te gustaría asistir como entrenador de estudiantes más jóvenes o quizá ocupar una hora a la semana brindando tu ayuda a algún compañero de equipo que está batallando con sus habilidades? Si a ti te gustan los niños, piensa en la posibilidad de ayudar con el programa para cuidar niños durante la Misa o entretener a los pequeños de tu colonia después de las horas de escuela.
>
> **¿Qué tipo de compromisos tienes en tu horario?** El fin del proyecto de servicio no es añadir más preocupaciones a tu vida o a la vida de tus papás. Considera aquellas ideas que sí pueden llevarse a cabo y son realistas. Si tu vida ya está muy llena de actividades, podrías considerar dejar a un lado algunas actividades que no están sirviendo para añadir calidad a tu vida. Esto podría ser un servicio a ti mismo y a tu familia.

Considera aquellos servicios que te gustaría continuar después de haber recibido el sacramento de la Confirmación. Recuerda que la Confirmación requiere que nos adentremos más en la vida de la Iglesia. Debemos **cambiar nuestros corazones** y llegar a ser jóvenes que lleven una vida de servicio, no solo cuando es útil, sino más bien, cuando es necesario.

La cosa más maravillosa acerca del servicio es que la recompensa es enorme. Cuando servimos a los demás, estamos amando, dejamos de estar encerrados en nosotros mismos, nos enfocamos menos en nuestros propios gustos. **Mientras más servimos a los demás, más amamos.** Eventualmente ambos se convierten en un modo de vida. Las personas que sirven están llenas de alegría, de paz y, en su servicio, llegan a ver el rostro de Dios.

ACTIVITY FOR THE FAMILY

When thinking about possible service projects, it will likely be helpful to get some input from your parents and loved ones. Chances are, they know you well and might have some good ideas on how to incorporate your **God-given talents** and interests into a Christian service project. From a practical standpoint, your parents will likely be the ones responsible for your transportation and scheduling, so demands on their time and resources are important considerations. Ultimately, the decision on how you want to serve your brothers and sisters is yours—but take time to talk about the following possible service projects and the ideas you come up with on your own.

Remember, **many opportunities await you** beyond your immediate circle of friends and immediate neighborhoods. People with needs live throughout the city, the nation, and the entire world. Service is a way of life!

IN YOUR HOMES AND NEIGHBORHOODS

- Prepare dinner for your family or for a family going through difficult times one day a week.
- Offer to take care of the younger children in your family so your parents can have a night out.
- Take special interest in an elderly person in your neighborhood and help him or her keep up the property by doing jobs that have become too difficult to handle.
- Organize young children in your neighborhood into a "club" that will meet an hour or two each week to do educational activities.

IN YOUR CHURCH

- Become involved in a ministry by working on your skills as a reader, music minister, or minister of hospitality. These are wonderful ways to become truly involved in the life of your parish.
- Promote and become actively involved in your parish youth group.
- Volunteer to baby-sit for parish service organizations such as choir rehearsals or parish council meetings.
- Become involved in those organizations within your parish that serve the poor.

IN YOUR CITY OR TOWN

- Volunteer at a hospital or nursing home and attempt to develop relationships with patients/residents who have few visitors.
- Involve yourself in local food drives, clothing/toy drives, or work projects that benefit the poor of your community.
- Volunteer to assist with coaching after-school sports programs that benefit children with special needs.
- Tutor younger students who are struggling with one or more of the "three R's."

IN THE NATION AND THE WORLD

- Educate yourself about current social justice issues. Become informed and involved in organizations that promote peace and justice.
- Promote the idea that we are stewards of the earth and support organizations that strive to protect our environment. Make an effort to become less wasteful and recycle everything that can possibly be reused.
- Develop a "pen-pal" relationship with someone who can **expand your point of view** or perhaps open your eyes to a whole new world, such as a person of your age who lives in another country, a prison inmate, or a missionary working far from home.

Finally, write down a few ideas that especially interest you.

TAREA EN FAMILIA

Al momento de pensar en posibles proyectos de servicio, sería bueno que escucharas las recomendaciones de tus papás. Es muy probable que ellos te conozcan muy bien y puedan darte buenas ideas de cómo aprovechar en proyectos de servicio **los talentos que Dios te ha dado** y también tus propios intereses. Desde un punto de vista práctico, tus padres serán los responsables del transporte y de tu horario, entonces, es bueno que se tomen en cuenta sus recursos y su tiempo.

Por último, la decisión de cómo quieres servir a tus hermanos y hermanas está en tus manos. Tómate el tiempo para hablar de los posibles proyectos de servicio y de las ideas que surgieron por tu cuenta. Recuerda que **hay muchas oportunidades** esperándote fuera del círculo cercano de amigos y vecinos. Hay personas con necesidades que viven en toda la ciudad, en todo el país y en el mundo entero. El servicio es un estilo de vida.

EN TU CASA Y EN TU COLONIA

- Prepara la cena para tu familia o para alguna familia que esté pasando por momentos difíciles, una vez por semana.
- Ofrécete para cuidar a tus hermanos pequeños, de modo que tus papás puedan tener una noche para salir juntos.
- Interésate por una persona anciana de tu colonia. Ayúdale a cuidar su casa y a realizar aquellas labores que se han vuelto imposibles para ella.
- Organiza un club con un grupo de niños de tu colonia, el cual se pueda reunir una o dos veces por semana para actividades educativas.

EN TU IGLESIA

- Involúcrate en un ministerio dentro de la parroquia. Mejora tus habilidades como lector, músico o encargado de acoger a nuevos miembros. Estos son modos maravillosos de participar en la vida de tu parroquia.
- Promueve y conviértete en un miembro activo del grupo de jóvenes de tu parroquia.
- Ofrécete para cuidar a los niños de aquellos que asisten a servicios en la parroquia, como son el coro o alguna reunión.
- Involúcrate en aquellas organizaciones que promueven, dentro de tu parroquia, el servicio a los pobres.

EN TU CIUDAD O POBLACIÓN

- Haz voluntariado en los hospitales o asilos de ancianos, e intenta llevar una relación con los pacientes o residentes que reciban pocas visitas.
- Participa en donaciones de comida, ropa, juguetes o en proyectos en beneficio de los pobres de tu comunidad.
- Ofrécete, después de la escuela, como asistente en los entrenamientos deportivos que benefician a niños con necesidades especiales.
- Ofrece tutoría a estudiantes más pequeños que estén batallando con una o más de sus materias.

EN TU PAÍS O EN EL MUNDO

- Estudia los asuntos actuales de justicia social. Infórmate e involúcrate en organizaciones que promuevan la paz y la justicia.
- Promueve la idea de que somos administradores de la Tierra y apoya a las organizaciones que luchan por proteger el medio ambiente. Haz un esfuerzo para desperdiciar menos y reciclar todo lo que se pueda volver a usar.
- Desarrolla una relación epistolar con alguien que pueda e**xpandir tu visión** o quizá te pueda abrir los ojos a un mundo totalmente nuevo para ti; por ejemplo, alguien de tu misma edad que viva en otro país, un prisionero o un misionero que trabaje lejos de casa.

Por último, anota algunas ideas que te llamen la atención de forma particular:

____

____

Basado en el texto original escrito por Michael Ketterhagen. Un agradecimiento especial a los padres Paul Niemann y Joe Kempf. Editado por Marco Batta. Diseño de Maggie Bubenik. ©2013 Libros Liguori, Liguori, MO 63057-9999.

Publicado con aprobación eclesiástica. Textos tomados del *Ritual para la Confirmación*, Editorial Buena Prensa 1999. Impreso en Estados Unidos.

Las citas de la Escritura están tomadas de la *Biblia Latinoamérica*, disponible en www.sobicain.org. Usada con permiso.

LIBROS LIGUORI™

Based on the original by Michael Ketterhagen. Special thanks to Rev. Paul Niemann and Rev. Joe Kempf. Edited by Lauren K. Borstell. Design by Maggie Bubenik.

©2013 Liguori Publications, Liguori, MO 63057-9999.

Published with ecclesiastical approval. Compliant with *The Roman Missal*, third edition. Printed in U.S.A.

Scripture quotation is taken from the *New Revised Standard Version Bible*, © 1989, Division of Christian Education of the National Council of Churches of Christ in the United States of America. Reprinted with permission.

Durante la ceremonia de Confirmación, el obispo extiende sus manos sobre los candidatos y ora así:

"Dios Todopoderoso, Padre de nuestro Señor Jesucristo, que regeneraste, por el agua y el Espíritu Santo, a estos siervos tuyos y los libraste del pecado: escucha nuestra oración y envía sobre ellos el Espíritu Santo Paráclito; llénalos de espíritu de sabiduría y de inteligencia, de espíritu de consejo y de fortaleza, de espíritu de ciencia y de piedad; y cólmalos del espíritu de tu santo temor. Por Jesucristo nuestro Señor" (Ritual de la Confirmación, 25).

¿POR QUÉ EL ESPÍRITU SANTO NOS OTORGA ESTOS DONES?

El Catecismo de la Iglesia Católica subraya algunos puntos en la descripción de los dones del Espíritu Santo. Primero, nos dice que los dones "pertenecen en plenitud a Cristo" (*CIC* 1831). En otras palabras, mientras nosotros hacemos uso de estos dones, vamos haciéndonos más como Cristo. Segundo, el Catecismo explica que los dones del Espíritu Santo "completan y llevan a su perfección las virtudes de quienes los reciben" (*CIC* 1831). Esta declaración implica que Dios al crearnos nos colmó de bondad y virtud, verdaderamente a su imagen y semejanza. El Espíritu, por su parte, nos ayuda a desarrollar y perfeccionar su bondad por medio de estos dones, pues "todos aquellos a los que guía el Espíritu de Dios son hijos e hijas de Dios" (Rom 8:14).

Otro punto importante que debe recalcarse acerca de los dones del Espíritu Santo es que estos dones no se conceden únicamente para la felicidad de la persona que los recibe. Son concedidos para el bien de una parroquia entera, para el bien de la Iglesia entera y para el bien de todo el mundo. Los dones del Espíritu Santo son concedidos para edificar el Cuerpo de Cristo y hacerlo santo. El Cuerpo de Cristo se hace santo porque estos dones fortalecen a los cristianos para que den testimonio de Cristo. Estos dones permiten al Pueblo de Dios vivir como Jesús. Los dones del Espíritu Santo nos dan a todos lo necesario para ser miembros activos y participar en la vida cristiana.

LOS FRUTOS DEL ESPÍRITU SANTO

En la carta de san Pablo a los Gálatas leemos: "el fruto del Espíritu es caridad, alegría, paz, comprensión de los demás, generosidad, bondad, fidelidad" (Gal 5:22-23). En otras palabras, cuando nos involucramos de lleno en la edificación del Reino de Dios en este mundo, cosechamos los frutos de nuestro arduo trabajo y maduración personal. Utilizando las Escrituras como referencia, la tradición de la Iglesia ha transmitido doce frutos del Espíritu Santo, estos son: "caridad, gozo, paz, paciencia, longanimidad, bondad, benignidad, mansedumbre, fidelidad, modestia, continencia, castidad (uso apropiado del don de la sexualidad)" (*CIC* 1832).

Cuando somos sellados con el don del Espíritu Santo, damos inicio a un nuevo camino de crecimiento hacia la madurez cristiana. Con la ayuda de los dones del Espíritu, podemos vivir una vida humana y cristiana plena. Podemos, así mismo, llegar a ser personas amables, humildes y llenas de paz.

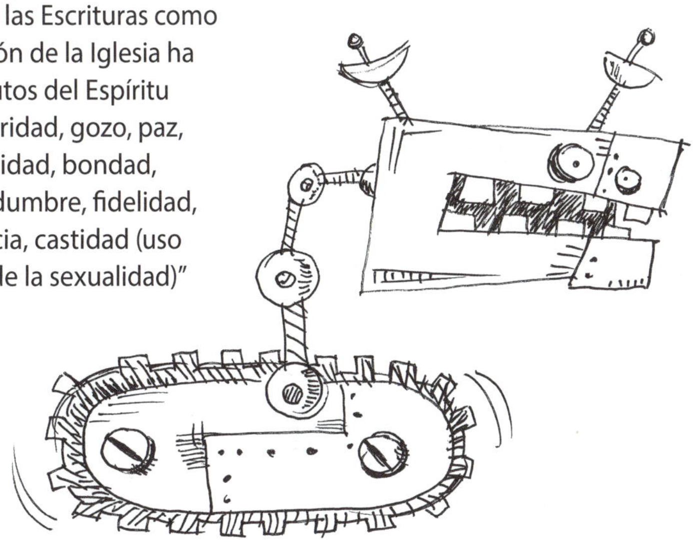

ACTIVITY FOR THE FAMILY

While you have ended each of your lessons thus far with activities involving your family, this small assignment **is best done alone** in a place that will allow for some quiet reflection. Before you begin this assignment, give your parents or loved ones a chance to review this lesson so that they may better understand what you are learning in your confirmation preparation. Then **seek out a quiet place** and reflect on the following:

As realistically as possible, assess "the state" of your life. **Are you basically a happy person**, or do you feel you spend too much time in periods of sadness or depression? Do you have a sense of peace and confidence in your relationships with others, or do you too often feel threatened, insecure, jealous, or angry? Do you have a faith in God that allows you to think positively about the future, or do you feel overwhelmed by pessimism and gloom? Carefully reflect on each of the gifts of the Holy Spirit—how will each help you to perfect the good qualities that are already a part of you? Then **focus on ONE gift** that is especially important to YOU in your life today. Compose a short prayer in which you ask the Holy Spirit for that gift. You might explain why you believe a particular gift would be especially valuable to you at this time. Share your prayer with your family or loved ones if you would like to do so.

MY PRAYER TO THE HOLY SPIRIT

TAREA EN FAMILIA

Si bien todas las lecciones pasadas han finalizado con una tarea que requería trabajar con tu familia, esta tarea en particular la podrás realizar **tú mismo** en un lugar que te permita realizar una reflexión tranquila.

Antes de iniciar esta tarea permite que tus papás o seres queridos se enteren de esta tarea y puedan saber lo que estás aprendiendo en tu preparación para la Confirmación. En seguida, **busca un lugar tranquilo** y reflexiona acerca de lo siguiente: Del modo más realista posible, evalúa el estado de tu vida. ¿Te consideras **una persona feliz** o crees que pasas mucho tiempo en estado de tristeza o depresión? ¿Posees un sentido de paz y confianza en tu relación con los demás o con frecuencia te sientes amenazado, inseguro, celoso o molesto? ¿Tienes confianza en Dios, lo que te permite ver positivamente el futuro o te sientes atrapado en el pesimismo y la tristeza? Reflexiona cuidadosamente en cada uno de los dones del Espíritu Santo. ¿De qué modo cada uno de estos dones te ayudará a perfeccionar las cualidades buenas que ya son parte de ti? Después, **enfócate en uno de los dones** que tenga mayor importancia en tu vida. Redacta una breve oración en la que pidas al Espíritu Santo ese don. Sería bueno que dieras una explicación de por qué ese don particular tiene un valor tan especial para ti en este momento. Si así lo deseas, comparte esta oración con tu familia y seres queridos.

MI ORACIÓN AL ESPÍRITU SANTO

Basado en el texto original escrito por Michael Ketterhagen. Un agradecimiento especial a los padres Paul Niemann y Joe Kempf. Editado por Marco Batta. Diseño de Maggie Bubenik.

Publicado con aprobación eclesiástica. Textos tomados del *Ritual para la Confirmación*, Editorial Buena Prensa 1999. Impreso en Estados Unidos.

LIBROS™ LIGUORI

Based on the original by Michael Ketterhagen. Special thanks to Rev. Paul Niemann and Rev. Joe Kempf. Edited by Lauren K. Borstell. Design by Maggie Bubenik.

Published with ecclesiastical approval. Compliant with *The Roman Missal*, third edition. Printed in U.S.A.

CIC 1303: Por este hecho, la Confirmación otorga crecimiento y profundidad a la gracia bautismal:

- nos introduce más profundamente en la filiación divina que nos hace decir "Abbá, Padre";
- nos une más firmemente a Cristo;
- aumenta en nosotros los dones del Espíritu Santo;
- hace más perfecto nuestro vínculo con la Iglesia;
- nos concede una fuerza especial del Espíritu Santo para difundir y defender la fe mediante la palabra y las obras, como verdaderos testigos de Cristo, de tal manera que podamos confesar valientemente el nombre de Cristo y que no sintamos jamás vergüenza de la cruz.

CIC 1304: La Confirmación, como el Bautismo del que es la plenitud, solo se da una vez. La Confirmación, en efecto, imprime en el alma *una marca espiritual indeleble*, el "carácter", que es el signo de que Jesucristo ha marcado al cristiano con el sello de su Espíritu revistiéndolo de la fuerza de lo alto para que sea su testigo.

La gran devoción de la Iglesia Católica al Espíritu Santo, tiene sus raíces en la Sagrada Escritura. Los autores del libro del Génesis, primer libro del Antiguo Testamento, eran conscientes del indescriptible poder creativo del Espíritu. Ellos se refieren a este poder en el primer pasaje de la Escritura: "En el principio, cuando Dios creó los cielos y la tierra, todo era confusión y no había nada en la tierra. Las tinieblas cubrían los abismos mientras **el espíritu de Dios aleteaba sobre la superficie de las aguas**" (Gn 1:1-2).

En el vocabulario hebreo existe una palabra, RUAH, que significa "viento", "aliento" y "espíritu". Las diversas traducciones al inglés varían principalmente en el modo en que interpretan el término; sin embargo, en todas las traducciones los versículos de la Escritura nos dicen que el poder creador del Espíritu Santo *estaba presente y activo al inicio de la Creación.*

La palabra *RUAH* aparece de nuevo en Génesis 2:7: "Entonces Yavé Dios formó al hombre con polvo de la tierra; luego sopló en su nariz un aliento de vida y el hombre tuvo aliento y vida". El Espíritu de Dios está tan cerca de nosotros como lo está nuestro aliento. En verdad, **Dios nos hizo a su imagen y semejanza**, *y después exhaló en nosotros su vida divina y su espíritu.*

El mismo Espíritu que aleteó sobre las aguas al inicio de la creación, también se posó sobre Jesús y permaneció como su inspiración durante toda su vida pública. En el evangelio de Lucas, Jesús nos dice:

"EL ESPÍRITU DEL SEÑOR ESTÁ SOBRE MÍ. ÉL ME HA UNGIDO PARA LLEVAR BUENAS NOTICIAS A LOS POBRES, PARA ANUNCIAR LA LIBERTAD A LOS CAUTIVOS Y A LOS CIEGOS QUE PRONTO VAN A VER, PARA PONER EN LIBERTAD A LOS OPRIMIDOS Y PROCLAMAR EL AÑO DE GRACIA DEL SEÑOR"

(LC 4:18-19).

Jesús no nos manda solos al mundo para realizar su obra. En la Confirmación somos marcados *con el mismo Espíritu Santo.* En la Confirmación celebramos nuestra aceptación del don del Espíritu de Jesús y nos comprometemos a ser miembros activos de la Iglesia.

ACTIVITY FOR THE FAMILY

An understanding of the Holy Spirit requires faith and the acceptance of **"mystery"** in our lives. The Spirit cannot be described in human terms. Even the "inspired" authors of the Bible could only use words like "wind," "breath," and "spirit."

Yet, chances are, each of us has somehow experienced the power and workings of the Holy Spirit. Take a few minutes with the other members of your family. Can you recall instances when you felt the power of the Holy Spirit at work in your lives? (Do not search for grand examples—most often the influence of the Spirit is subtle.)

On the lines below, **briefly record** a single instance when you believe the Holy Spirit was instrumental in your life, or in the life of your family, or even in the life of your faith community. (Recall the grace of a special friendship, the healing of wounds within family relationships, the feeling of "oneness" experienced by church members as they praise God through the singing of a special hymn.) As always, after you record your thoughts, post this page in a place where you will come across it often in the next week. **Try to be especially aware of the work of the Spirit in your life** and in the lives of your friends and loved ones throughout the week.

TAREA EN FAMILIA

Entender al Espíritu Santo requiere la fe y la aceptación del **"misterio"** en nuestras vidas. El Espíritu no puede ser descrito en términos humanos. Incluso los autores inspirados de la Biblia solo pudieron usar términos como "viento", "aliento" y "espíritu".

Aun así, es posible que cada uno de nosotros haya experimentado el poder y la obra del Espíritu Santo. Toma algunos minutos con los otros miembros de tu familia. ¿Puedes recordar momentos en los que sentiste el poder del Espíritu Santo trabajando en tu vida? No busques grandes momentos, dado que muchas veces el influjo del Espíritu es imperceptible.

En las líneas de abajo **describe brevemente** un momento en el que tu creíste que el Espíritu Santo estaba presente en tu vida, en la vida de tu familia o incluso en la vida de la comunidad de fe (recuerda la gracia de una amistad especial, la gracia de sanar una herida con la ayuda de alguna relación familiar, el sentimiento de unidad experimentado por los miembros de la Iglesia durante la adoración a Dios por medio de algún canto especial). Como siempre, después de haber escrito tus pensamientos, colócalos en un lugar donde puedas verlos continuamente a lo largo de la siguiente semana. **Intenta tener muy presente durante esta semana el trabajo del Espíritu en tu vida** y en la vida de tus amigos y seres queridos.

Basado en el texto original escrito por Michael Ketterhagen. Un agradecimiento especial a los padres Paul Niemann y Joe Kempf. Editado por Marco Batta. Diseño de Maggie Bubenik.

Publicado con aprobación eclesiástica. Textos tomados del Ritual para la Confirmación, Editorial Buena Prensa 1999. Impreso en Estados Unidos.

Las citas de la Escritura están tomadas de la *Biblia Latinoamérica*, disponible en www.sobicain.org.

Based on the original by Michael Ketterhagen. Special thanks to Rev. Paul Niemann and Rev. Joe Kempf. Edited by Lauren K. Borstell. Design by Maggie Bubenik.

Published with ecclesiastical approval. Compliant with *The Roman Missal*, third edition. Printed in U.S.A.

estaba marcado por un sentido de conversión constante a través de la Palabra de Dios, la oración frecuente y periodos regulares de ayuno y obras de caridad. El periodo de los catecúmenos **era en verdad un tiempo espiritual profundo**.

Aquellos candidatos que estaban ya listos para recibir el Bautismo, eran elegidos al inicio de la Cuaresma, para prepararse a su celebración de iniciación. La comunidad entera oraba frecuentemente por ellos.

Por último, en la madrugada de la mañana de Pascua, los candidatos eran conducidos a la piscina para el Bautismo y eran sumergidos en el agua mientras profesaban su fe en el Padre, en el Hijo y en el Espíritu Santo. Los recién bautizados eran confirmados por el obispo con el don del Espíritu, por medio de la imposición de las manos y la unción. La nueva comunidad de miembros completaba su iniciación llevando al altar los dones del pan y del vino, y compartiendo la Eucaristía con la comunidad cristiana **por primera vez**.

Esta experiencia intensa de conversión en medio de la comunidad, era seguida de otro periodo de instrucción que duraba los cincuenta días de la Pascua, hasta Pentecostés.

EDAD MEDIA Y TIEMPOS MODERNOS

Pero las cosas iban cambiando. A medida que el cristianismo se convertía en la religión oficial del mundo occidental, disminuyeron las conversiones de adultos. La mayoría de las personas pertenecían a la Iglesia desde su infancia, desde el momento de su Bautismo. La Confirmación tenía lugar antes de la Primera Comunión, la cual **se celebraba a los doce años**. La presencia del obispo recordaba a los candidatos que ellos eran miembros de la Iglesia entera, no solo de su pequeña comunidad de fe. Durante la Edad media, la Confirmación, al estar separada del Bautismo, comenzó a tener otras características de iniciación. La Confirmación llegó a ser conocida como el sacramento por el que uno se convertía en "soldado de Cristo". La experiencia misma de la Confirmación resaltaba el "testimonio cristiano", simbolizado en el suave golpe que el obispo daba en la mejilla del candidato.

LOS CAMBIOS DEL SIGLO XX

En el siglo XX, **un cambio grande** ocurrió en el proceso de iniciación. El Papa Pío X quería que los niños recibieran la Eucaristía antes. Así fueron introducidos en la práctica de la Primera Comunión a la edad en que ya tenían "uso de razón", más o menos a los siete u ocho años. Sin embargo, la Confirmación seguía recibiéndose a la edad de doce años en la mayoría de las diócesis. Esto significa que se había alterado el orden tradicional de los sacramentos de iniciación –Bautismo, Confirmación y Eucaristía. Este cambio en el orden en que se reciben estos tres sacramentos importantes, ha creado mucho debate y discusión dentro de la Iglesia Católica. Líderes de la Iglesia y académicos están luchando por aclarar el significado y propósito de la Confirmación hoy en día. ¿Se trata más de un sacramento de iniciación que de un sacramento de compromiso? El estudio y discusión del tema sigue en pie actualmente.

El Vaticano II ordenó que se revisara el rito de la Confirmación, de modo que expresara de manera más clara el significado y lugar de este sacramento en la vida cristiana. **El nuevo rito** enfatiza la unidad entre el Bautismo, la Confirmación y la Eucaristía. Para mostrar la relación entre el Bautismo y la Confirmación, se pide a la persona que está por ser confirmada, que renueve sus promesas bautismales. La unidad entre la Confirmación y la Eucaristía está resaltada por el hecho de que la Confirmación se lleva a cabo dentro de la Misa. En efecto, se celebra una Misa especial en la que las oraciones y lecturas se centran en el significado de la Confirmación.

El énfasis en la responsabilidad compartida de la parroquia o de la comunidad en la celebración de la Confirmación es otro rasgo importante del nuevo rito. La celebración del sacramento ya no se considera como un asunto personal que tiene interés solamente para aquellos que van a ser confirmados, para sus padrinos y para los papás. **La totalidad del Pueblo de Dios**, representada por la comunidad local, es invitada a tomar parte y a regocijarse con motivo de la recepción del don del Espíritu Santo en sus miembros.

ACTIVITY FOR THE FAMILY

Read together the following excerpt from the *Apostolic Constitution on the Sacrament of Confirmation*:

***In baptism**, the newly baptized receive forgiveness of sins, adoption as sons and daughters of God, and the character of Christ, by which they are made members of the Church and for the first time become sharers in the priesthood of their Savior (see 1 Peter 2:5,9). Through the sacrament of confirmation, those who have been born anew in baptism receive the inexpressible Gift, the Holy Spirit.... Moreover,...they are "bound more intimately to the Church" and "they are more strictly obliged to spread and defend the faith both by word and by deed as true witnesses of Christ" (Ad Gentes No. 11: AAS, 58-959-960). Finally, confirmation is so closely linked with the holy Eucharist that the faithful, after being signed by holy baptism and confirmation, are incorporated fully into the body of Christ by participation in the Eucharist.*

This excerpt makes it clear that Catholicism is not a "passive" religion. Each of us is asked to participate in the life of our Church, each according to his or her own gifts and abilities.

With the adult members of your family, discuss ways in which you could become more active in your parish, faith community, or diocese. Carefully consider your own talents, gifts, and interests. Do not overcommit yourself. Think simply and realistically. On the lines below, write down some possible ways you could become more involved in the lives of God's people:

____

____

____

____

____

____

POST THESE IDEAS IN A PLACE WHERE YOU WILL SEE THEM OFTEN DURING THE FOLLOWING WEEK—AND CONSIDER THEM CAREFULLY.

TAREA EN FAMILIA

Lean juntos los siguientes extractos de la *Constitución Apostólica sobre el Sacramento de la Confirmación*:

***En el Bautismo**, los neófitos reciben el perdón de los pecados, la adopción como hijos de Dios y el carácter de Cristo, por el cual quedan agregados a la Iglesia y se hacen partícipes inicialmente del sacerdocio de su Salvador (cfr. 1 Pe 2:5,9). Con el sacramento de la Confirmación los renacidos en el Bautismo reciben un don inefable, el Espíritu Santo mismo… es más… "quedan vinculados más perfectamente a la Iglesia", "a la vez que quedan más estrictamente obligados a difundir y defender la propia fe con la palabra y las obras, como auténticos testigos de Cristo" (Ad Gentes divinitus, n. 11: AAS, 58-959-960). Finalmente, la Confirmación está tan vinculada a la Eucaristía, que los fieles, marcados ya por el Bautismo y la Confirmación, quedan de manera plena en el Cuerpo de Cristo mediante la participación de la Eucaristía.*

Este extracto deja claro que el catolicismo no es una religión pasiva. A cada uno de nosotros se nos pide que participemos en la vida de la Iglesia, de acuerdo con los propios dones y habilidades.

Discute con los miembros adultos de tu familia algunos modos en los que podrías ser un miembro activo en tu parroquia, en la comunidad de fe o en la diócesis. Considera con cuidado tus talentos, dones e intereses. No te llenes de compromisos. Piensa de modo simple y realista. Escribe en las líneas de abajo algunas formas posibles en las que puedas involucrarte más en la vida del Pueblo de Dios:

____

____

____

____

____

____

COLOCA ESTAS IDEAS EN UN LUGAR DONDE PUEDAS VERLAS CONTINUAMENTE DURANTE LA SEMANA Y REFLEXIONA EN ELLAS CUIDADOSAMENTE.

Basado en el texto original escrito por Michael Ketterhagen. Un agradecimiento especial a los padres Paul Niemann y Joe Kempf. Editado por Marco Batta. Diseño de Maggie Bubenik.

Publicado con aprobación eclesiástica. Textos tomados del Ritual para la Confirmación, Editorial Buena Prensa 1999. Impreso en Estados Unidos.

LIBROS LIGUORI™

Based on the original by Michael Ketterhagen. Special thanks to Rev. Paul Niemann and Rev. Joe Kempf. Edited by Lauren K. Borstell. Design by Maggie Bubenik.

Published with ecclesiastical approval. Compliant with *The Roman Missal*, third edition. Printed in U.S.A.

EL SÍMBOLO DE LOS APÓSTELES

El símbolo de los Apóstoles, la primera oración del Rosario, es otra declaración de fe de la Iglesia.

Creo en Dios,
Padre todopoderoso,
Creador del Cielo y de la Tierra.
Creo en Jesucristo, su único Hijo,
Nuestro Señor,
que fue concebido por obra y
gracia del Espíritu Santo,
nació de Santa María Virgen,
padeció bajo el poder de
Poncio Pilato,
fue crucificado,
muerto y sepultado,
descendió a los infiernos,
al tercer día resucitó de entre
los muertos,
subió a los cielos
y está sentado a la derecha
de Dios, Padre todopoderoso.
Desde allí ha de venir a
juzgar a vivos y muertos.
Creo en el Espíritu Santo,
la santa Iglesia Católica,
la comunión de los santos,
el perdón de los pecados,
la resurrección de la carne
y la vida eterna.
Amén.

LOS DIEZ MANDAMIENTOS

Además de las dos declaraciones de los credos, que son las declaraciones de doctrina básica de la comunidad católica, hay dos directrices basadas en la Escritura y que forman parte de los estándares de vida moral de los cristianos. El primero de estos pasajes de la Escritura se encuentra en el libro del Éxodo 20:1-7:

UNO Yo soy Yavé, tu Dios, el que te sacó de Egipto, país de esclavitud. No tendrás otros dioses fuera de mí. No te harás estatua ni imagen alguna de lo que hay arriba, en el cielo, abajo, en la tierra, y en las aguas debajo de la tierra. No te postres ante esos dioses, ni les sirvas, porque yo, Yavé, tu Dios, soy un Dios celoso. Yo pido cuentas a hijos, nietos y biznietos por la maldad de sus padres que no me quisieron. Pero me muestro favorable hasta mil generaciones con los que me aman y observan mis mandamientos.

DOS No tomarás en vano el nombre de Yavé, tu Dios, porque Yavé no dejará sin castigo a aquel que toma su nombre en vano.

TRES Acuérdate del día del Sábado, para santificarlo. Trabaja seis días y, en ellos haz todas tus tareas. Pero el día séptimo es día de descanso, consagrado a Yavé, tu Dios. Que nadie trabaje: ni tú, ni tus hijos, ni tus hijas, ni tus siervos, ni tus siervas, ni tus animales, ni los forasteros que viven en tu país. Pues en seis días Yavé hizo el cielo y la tierra, el mar y cuanto hay en ellos, y el séptimo día descansó. Por eso bendijo el Sábado y lo hizo sagrado.

CUATRO Respeta a tu padre y a tu madre, para que se prolongue tu vida sobre la tierra que Yavé, tu Dios, te da.

CINCO No matarás.

SEIS No cometerás adulterio.

SIETE No robarás.

OCHO No atestiguarás en falso contra tu prójimo.

NUEVE No codiciarás la casa de tu prójimo.

DIEZ No codiciarás a su mujer, ni a sus servidores, a su buey o a su burro. No codiciarás nada de lo que le pertenece.

THE EIGHT BEATITUDES

The second passage—called the Beatitudes—is found in Matthew's Gospel (5:3-12). These statements, unlike the Ten Commandments, focus on what we must do (rather than not do) if we wish to follow the teachings of Jesus. In many ways, the Beatitudes are very challenging to the Christian because they demand that we be active!

Blessed are the poor in spirit, for theirs is the kingdom of heaven.

Blessed are those who mourn, for they will be comforted.

Blessed are the meek, for they will inherit the earth.

Blessed are those who hunger and thirst for righteousness, for they will be filled.

Blessed are the merciful, for they will receive mercy.

Blessed are the pure in heart, for they will see God.

Blessed are the peacemakers, for they will be called children of God.

Blessed are those who are persecuted for righteousness' sake, for theirs is the kingdom of heaven.

Blessed are you when people revile you and persecute you and utter all kinds of evil against you falsely on my account. Rejoice and be glad, for your reward is great in heaven, for in the same way they persecuted the prophets who were before you.

THE BEATITUDES ARE VERY CHALLENGING TO THE CHRISTIAN BECAUSE THEY DEMAND THAT WE BE ACTIVE!

LAS OCHO BIENAVENTURANZAS

El segundo pasaje, llamado las Bienaventuranzas, se encuentra en el Evangelio de san Mateo 5:3-12. Estas declaraciones, al contario de los mandamientos, se centran en lo que debemos hacer, no en lo que no debemos hacer, si queremos seguir las enseñanzas de Jesús. Las Bienaventuranzas representan, de muchas maneras, un gran reto para los cristianos, dado que piden que seamos activos.

> **LAS BIENAVENTURANZAS REPRESENTAN, DE MUCHAS MANERAS, UN GRAN RETO PARA LOS CRISTIANOS, DADO QUE PIDEN QUE SEAMOS ACTIVOS.**

Felices los que tienen el espíritu del pobre, porque de ellos es el Reino de los Cielos.

Felices los que lloran, porque recibirán consuelo.

Felices los pacientes, porque recibirán la tierra en herencia.

Felices los que tienen hambre y sed de justicia, porque serán saciados.

Felices los compasivos, porque obtendrán misericordia.

Felices los de corazón limpio, porque verán a Dios.

Felices los que trabajan por la paz, porque serán reconocidos como hijos de Dios.

Felices los que son perseguidos por causa del bien, porque de ellos es el Reino de los Cielos.

Felices ustedes, cuando por causa mía, los insulten, los persigan y les levanten toda clase de calumnias.

Alégrense y muéstrense contentos, porque será grande la recompensa que recibirán en el Cielo. Pues bien saben que así persiguieron a los profetas que vinieron antes de ustedes.

Basado en el texto original escrito por Michael Ketterhagen. Un agradecimiento especial a los padres Paul Niemann y Joe Kempf. Editado por Marco Batta. Diseño de Maggie Bubenik. ©2013 Libros Liguori, Liguori, MO 63057-9999.

Publicado con aprobación eclesiástica. Textos tomados del Ritual para la Confirmación, Editorial Buena Prensa 1999. Impreso en Estados Unidos.

LIBROS LIGUORI™

Based on the original by Michael Ketterhagen. Special thanks to Rev. Paul Niemann and Rev. Joe Kempf. Edited by Lauren K. Borstell. Design by Maggie Bubenik.

Published with ecclesiastical approval. Compliant with *The Roman Missal*, third edition. Printed in U.S.A.

nosotros. Dios nos acepta y nos ama incondicionalmente. Como aprendimos en la primera lección, nuestro Bautismo revistió nuestro ser de un gran valor. El simple hecho de ser hijos de Dios representa la principal razón por la que merecemos ser queridos y amados.

EN LA CONFIRMACIÓN, POR LA FUERZA DEL ESPÍRITU, HACEMOS DE LA FE ALGO PROPIO

El Bautismo coloca a la persona en la fe de la Iglesia. Un bebé o niño pequeño es casi completamente pasivo. No obstante, la gracia de Dios, se le otorga gratuitamente. La Confirmación, tal y como se celebra en la actualidad, en gran parte es el momento activo del proceso de iniciación. El cristiano bautizado toma la fe que le fue dada y la hace propia. Un candidato a la Confirmación, después de haber revisado cuidadosamente lo que le Iglesia enseña, busca aceptar estas enseñanzas como algo propio. Con la aceptación debe venir una participación deliberada y activa en la vida de la fe comunitaria.

EN LA EUCARISTÍA SE NUTRE A NUESTRO ESPÍRITU

Otro nombre que se da a la Muerte y Resurrección de Jesús es el de Misterio Pascual. Jesús es el "Cordero de Dios". Él mismo permitió su muerte y, por medio de su sufrimiento y muerte en la cruz, nosotros podemos vivir. En la Eucaristía, se celebra el Misterio Pascual. Como respuesta al don que Cristo hace de sí mismo, nosotros traemos ante Él nuestras propias vidas, por medio de los símbolos del pan y del vino, "fruto del trabajo del hombre". Dios acepta nuestras vidas, las consagra y nutre nuestro espíritu por medio de su presencia en la Eucaristía.

PREGUNTAS PARA REFLEXIONAR

Tu preparación para recibir el sacramento de la Confirmación debe incluir un buen examen de conciencia. Es importante que te hagas las siguientes preguntas: ¿Qué significa para mí el Bautismo? ¿Qué significa tener vida dentro de la Iglesia?

Como ayuda para responder a estas preguntas difíciles, imagínate que nunca hubieras sido bautizado. Imagina que tus padres y padrinos nunca te hubieran introducido en la comunidad cristiana. Describe de modo detallado qué tan diferente sería tu vida. Por ejemplo, ¿qué clase de entorno moral tendrías si nunca hubieras conocido a Cristo?, ¿qué clase de amigos tendrías?, quizá irías a una escuela diferente. ¿Cómo celebrarías fechas especiales como la Navidad o la Pascua, si Jesús no fuera parte de tu vida? ¿Verías la muerte de modo diverso? Deseamos que, al ver tu vida desde esta perspectiva (sin los sacramentos de iniciación), seas capaz de reconocer y apreciar los diferentes modos en que los dones de la gracia de Dios influyen y tocan tu vida.

ACTIVITY FOR THE FAMILY

Select an adult or older sibling in your family and request that he or she grant you a short interview. Explain that you would like to learn how this person experienced the sacraments of initiation. (If none of the members of your immediate family are Catholic, you might need to call a friend or relative whom you know has received the sacraments.) Here are a few questions that can be used for your interview—but feel free to add your own, particularly if you are interviewing someone with an unusual or interesting faith background. Again, post your interview in a very visible place for a week or two. Reflect on the unique way we are each called to holiness.

Name of person interviewed:

____

Date:

____

Relationship:

____

How old were you when you were baptized?

____

If you were old enough to remember your baptism, what, specifically, do you most remember?

____

When were you confirmed? Describe your preparation for this sacrament. What aspects of confirmation were most emphasized during your study and preparation?

____

____

When did you first receive the Eucharist? What do you most remember about your first experience of this sacrament?

____

____

Are you still an active participant in the life of the Church today? If so, in what ways do you serve and benefit from your faith community?

____

____

TAREA EN FAMILIA

Elige a un familiar adulto o a uno de tus hermanos que sea mayor que tú y pídele que te conceda una breve entrevista. Explícale que te gustaría saber cuál fue su experiencia acerca de los sacramentos de iniciación. En caso de que ninguno de tus familiares cercanos sea católico, pide ayuda a un amigo o familiar que haya recibido los sacramentos. Aquí se exponen algunas preguntas que puedes hacer durante la entrevista. Siéntete libre de añadir tus propias preguntas, en especial si estás entrevistando a alguien que tenga una peculiar o inusual historia de fe. Una vez más, coloca tu entrevista en un lugar visible por una o dos semanas. Reflexiona acerca del modo único en el que todos somos llamados a la santidad.

Nombre de la persona entrevistada:

____

Fecha:

____

Relación:

____

¿Qué edad tenías cuando recibiste el Bautismo?

____

Si ya eras grande cuando fuiste bautizado, ¿qué recuerdas en especial de esa fecha?

____

¿Cuándo recibiste la Confirmación? Que describa su preparación para este sacramento. ¿Cuáles fueron los aspectos que más se resaltaban durante su estudio y preparación?

____

____

¿Cuándo recibiste la Primera Comunión? ¿Qué es lo que más recuerdas acerca de la primera experiencia de este sacramento?

____

____

¿Eres aún miembro activo de la vida de la Iglesia? De ser así, ¿de qué modo sirves y te beneficias de la comunidad de fe?

____

____

Basado en el texto original escrito por Michael Ketterhagen. Un agradecimiento especial a los padres Paul Niemann y Joe Kempf. Editado por Marco Batta. Diseño de Maggie Bubenik.

Publicado con aprobación eclesiástica. Textos tomados del Ritual para la Confirmación, Editorial Buena Prensa 1999. Impreso en Estados Unidos.

LIBROS LIGUORI™

Based on the original by Michael Ketterhagen. Special thanks to Rev. Paul Niemann and Rev. Joe Kempf. Edited by Lauren K. Borstell. Design by Maggie Bubenik.

Published with ecclesiastical approval. Compliant with *The Roman Missal*, third edition. Printed in U.S.A.

LAS PALABRAS DE COMPROMISO

A LOS CANDIDATOS PARA LA CONFIRMACIÓN

Celebrante: Dios los ha llamado a ser hijos e hijas de Dios por medio del sacramento del Bautismo. Ustedes han seguido la Luz. Ahora el camino del Evangelio se abre aún más ante ustedes, invitándolos a reconocer el amor de Dios por cada uno de ustedes al pedirles su compromiso para vivir una vida de servicio y amor, de paz y de justicia para todos. Este es el camino de la fe en el que Cristo los guiará de modo amoroso a la vida eterna. ¿Están ustedes listos para iniciar este viaje?

Candidatos: Sí, lo estoy.

Celebrante: ¿Están dispuestos a aceptar a la comunidad cristiana como el entorno en que llevarán a cabo su experiencia de fe y de crecimiento en el Espíritu?

Candidatos: Sí, lo estoy.

Celebrante: ¿Están dispuestos a profundizar en su compromiso personal con Jesucristo y a hacerse responsables de los dones del Espíritu, a fin de poder edificar el Reino de Dios?

Candidatos: Sí, lo estoy.

A LOS PADRINOS DE CONFIRMACIÓN

Celebrante: ¿Están dispuestos a ayudar a estos candidatos a llegar a la Confirmación en su viaje del Espíritu, en nombre de la comunidad cristiana?

Padrinos: Sí, lo estoy.

A LA COMUNIDAD PARROQUIAL

Celebrante: ¿Continuarán renovando su fe en el mismo espíritu de su Confirmación?

Comunidad: Sí, lo haremos.

Celebrante: ¿Apoyarán a estos jóvenes de su comunidad cristiana en el seguimiento de Jesús y de su Evangelio?

Comunidad: Sí, lo haremos.

Celebrante: Señor de amor y de bondad, te damos las gracias, en nombre de nuestros hermanos y hermanas, que han experimentado tu presencia en sus vidas. Hoy, en presencia de tu comunidad, van a prometer prepararse para tu venIda en el sacramento de la Confirmación *(ahora el celebrante pide a los padrinos que hagan el signo de la cruz sobre los candidatos para prepararlos a su viaje del Espíritu).*

Recibe la cruz de Cristo: por medio de este signo de amor, Cristo será tu fortaleza. Aprende ahora a conocerlo y a seguirlo. Él es tu fiel compañero, recuérdalo cuando estudies, cuando reflexiones, cuando te prepares y cuando ores.

Candidatos: Amén.

Celebrante: Señor, te pedimos por aquellos que han recibido el signo de la cruz de Nuestro Señor Jesucristo. Por su poder, guárdalos. Que sean fieles al llamado, para que puedan vivir con su amado Creador en la gloria. Te lo pedimos por Cristo, Señor nuestro.

Todos: Amén.

Sigue la oración de los fieles.

ACTIVITY FOR THE FAMILY

In this lesson, we have discussed the importance of the parish community as a source of support and strength as we strive to follow in the footsteps of our Lord Jesus. You have asked the parish family to pledge its prayers and support as you prepare to receive the sacrament of confirmation—and you have committed yourselves to study and prepare to the best of your abilities.

Now, you will seek a simple but important commitment from your own family—the promise to support you and pray for you as you seek to learn all you can about the sacrament you hope to receive in the coming months. Practically speaking, you are asking your family and loved ones to take your preparation very seriously, to assist you in finding adequate time for study and reflection, to be willing to review the lessons with you, and most importantly, to support you with their prayers.

Your families are likely the most influential members of the greater parish family in terms of your faith development, so their commitments are very helpful. Ask each member of your family (those old enough to understand) to read the following statement. If he or she is up to the challenge, he or she may sign below. Again, post this page in a place where you will see it often in the weeks ahead.

I PROMISE

to do my best to help confirmation candidate,

____

Name of Candidate

prepare to receive this sacrament through my encouragement, support, and prayers.

(signatures)

____

____

TAREA EN FAMILIA

En esta lección, hemos discutido la importancia que tiene la comunidad parroquial como fuente de apoyo y fortaleza en nuestra lucha para seguir las huellas de Nuestro Señor. Ustedes han pedido a la comunidad parroquial que eleve sus oraciones y su apoyo durante el tiempo de su preparación para el sacramento de la Confirmación. Ustedes, por su parte, se han comprometido a estudiar y a prepararse como mejor se lo permitan sus cualidades.

Ahora buscarás que tu familia haga un compromiso sencillo, pero a la vez importante. Puede ser la promesa de apoyarte y rezar por ti en tu preparación para que aprendas lo más que puedas acerca del sacramento que esperas recibir en los siguientes meses. De modo más sencillo, tú estás pidiendo que tu familia y seres queridos se tomen muy en serio tu preparación, que te asistan para encontrar un tiempo adecuado para tus estudios y para la reflexión, que estén listos para revisar las lecciones contigo y, lo que es más importante, que te apoyen con sus oraciones.

Tu familia es, sin lugar a dudas, el conjunto de miembros, dentro de toda la familia parroquial, que más ha influido en el desarrollo de tu fe. Por eso su compromiso es de suma importancia. Pide a cada miembro de tu familia (aquellos que por su edad puedan entender más) que lean la siguiente declaración. Si él o ella están a la altura del reto, lo firmarán. Una vez más, coloca esta hoja en un lugar donde lo puedas ver tan seguido como te sea posible en las siguientes semanas.

YO PROMETO

hacer mi mejor esfuerzo para ayudar a este candidato para la Confirmación,

____

Nombre del candidato

a prepararse para recibir este sacramento con mi estímulo, apoyo y oraciones.

Firmas

____

____

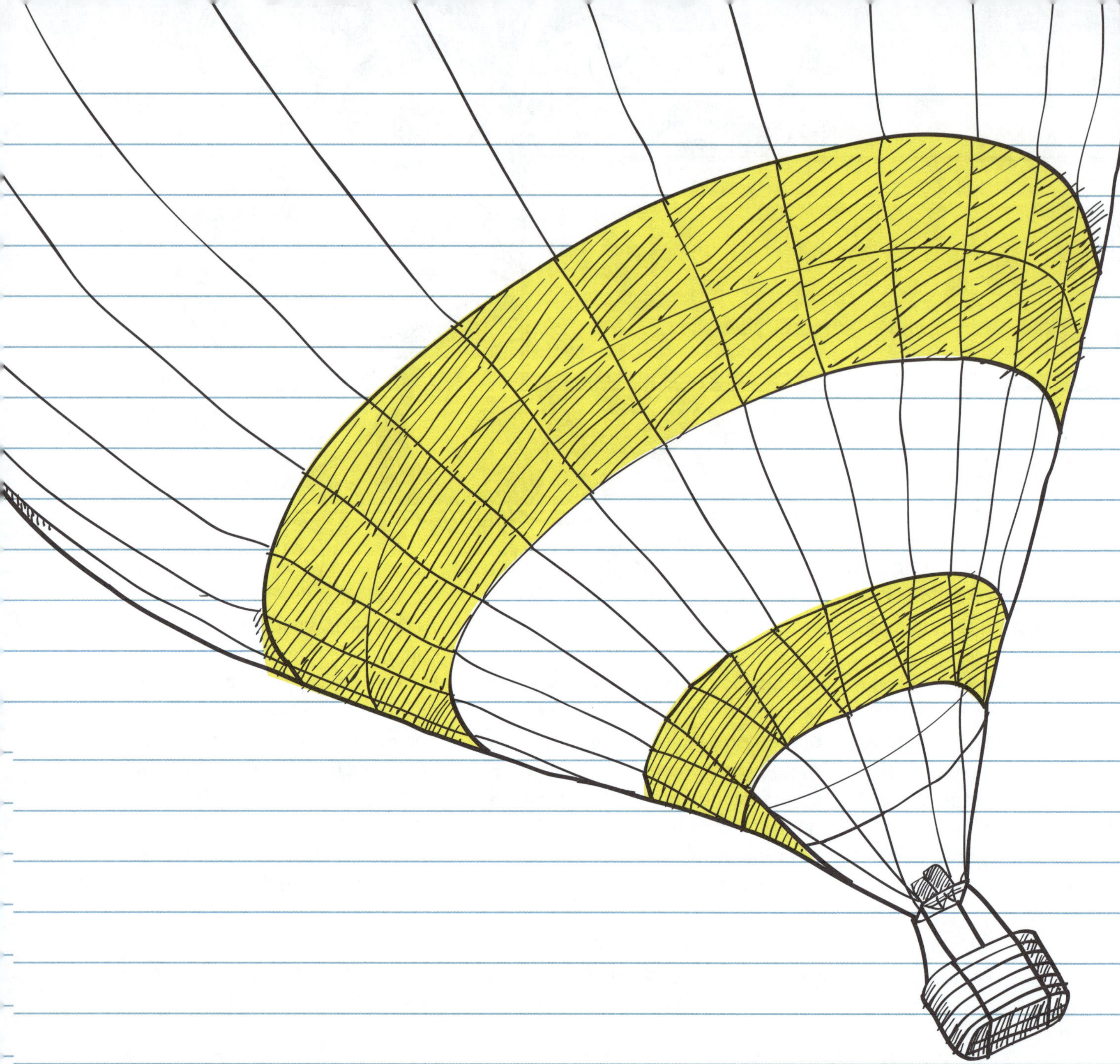

Basado en el texto original escrito por Michael Ketterhagen. Un agradecimiento especial a los padres Paul Niemann y Joe Kempf. Editado por Marco Batta. Diseño de Maggie Bubenik. ©2013 Libros Liguori, Liguori, MO 63057-9999.

Publicado con aprobación eclesiástica. Textos tomados del Ritual para la Confirmación, Editorial Buena Prensa 1999. Impreso en Estados Unidos.

Las citas de la Escritura están tomadas de la *Biblia Latinoamérica*, disponible en www.sobicain.org.

Based on the original by Michael Ketterhagen. Special thanks to Rev. Paul Niemann and Rev. Joe Kempf. Edited by Lauren K. Borstell. Design by Maggie Bubenik.

©2013 Liguori Publications, Liguori, MO 63057-9999.

Published with ecclesiastical approval. Compliant with *The Roman Missal*, third edition. Printed in U.S.A.

Scripture quotation is taken from the *New Revised Standard Version Bible*, © 1989, Division of Christian Education of the National Council of Churches of Christ in the United States of America. Reprinted with permission. All rights reserved.

La Iglesia Católica también nos ofrece la vida sacramental como camino para encontrar a Cristo. La Tradición ha definido el sacramento como un signo externo instituido por Cristo para dar la gracia. De un modo más sencillo, el sacramento es un momento especial de nuestra vida como católicos en el que signos externos y rituales nos conducen hacia una relación más íntima con Jesús. Por medio de ministros humanos, Jesús nos perdona, nos nutre, nos cura. Y en ese encuentro personal con Él recibimos también su fuerza para poder seguir sus huellas.

A través de los sacramentos recibimos la gracia, un don de Dios. No ganamos la gracia por nuestro esfuerzo o estudio. La gracia se recibe gratuitamente por la generosidad del Señor que desea fortalecernos mediante su maravilloso y misterioso influjo. Los sacramentos requieren fe, pues encierran un misterio.

Durante las siguientes semanas ustedes se adentrarán en la riqueza del sacramento de la Confirmación, sacramento que está ligado íntimamente al Bautismo. La Confirmación, como todos los otros sacramentos, comienza con un ritual, pero la gracia recibida se experimenta a cada paso de nuestro gran viaje.

PREGUNTAS PARA REFLEXIONAR

Ciertamente cuando nos bautizaron, éramos demasiado pequeños para recordar la maravilla de este sacramento por el cual fuimos recibidos y acogidos en la comunidad cristiana y llegamos a ser hijos de Dios. Uno de los objetivos de la Confirmación de adolescentes, es hacer conscientes a los jóvenes del sentido de dignidad y valor que brota precisamente de su Bautismo… pues, en efecto, ellos son hijos queridos de Dios. Recordar nuestro Bautismo nos ayuda a reflexionar en el gran valor que poseemos cuando probablemente estamos dudando de ello.

PREGUNTAS PARA REFLEXIONAR

- ¿Qué significa ser "hijo de Dios"?
- ¿Qué significado tiene tu Bautismo actualmente?
- El óleo (crisma) de nuestro Bautismo nos recuerda que somos "sacerdotes, profetas y reyes" (*Orden del bautismo de niños*). Aun así, nuestra sociedad define nuestros valores de forma destructiva. ¿Puedes dar uno o dos ejemplos de cómo nuestra sociedad define nuestros valores?

(Recuerda "Los caminos de éxito" discutidos antes en esta lección)

ACTIVITY FOR THE FAMILY

With the help of your parents or other loved ones, recall the day of your baptism. Record a few important details.

Date of your baptism:

___

Your godparents:

___

Place where you were baptized:

___

Your age at the time of your baptism:

___

Family members and important loved ones present to witness your baptism:

___

___

If it is possible, find a picture of yourself taken on the day of your baptism. Tape it to this paper in the space below. Hang it on your refrigerator or in some other prominent place. Over the course of the week, every time you see this paper, thank God for the gifts of life and grace received through baptism—and then remind yourself of how very much you are loved by your Creator God.

TAREA EN FAMILIA

Con la ayuda de tus papás o algún ser querido, recuerda el día de tu Bautismo. Toma nota de algunos detalles importantes.

¿Cuál fue el día de tu Bautismo?

¿Quiénes fueron tus padrinos?

¿Dónde te bautizaron?

¿Qué edad tenías cuando fuiste bautizado?

¿Qué miembros de tu familia y qué seres queridos estaban presentes en la ceremonia?

Si es posible, busca una foto tuya del día de tu Bautismo. Pégala en este papel, en el espacio que está debajo de este párrafo. Pégalo en el refrigerador o en algún otro lugar visible. Durante la semana, cada vez que veas esta hoja, agradece a Dios por el don de la vida y de la gracia recibida por medio del Bautismo; en seguida, recuerda lo mucho que Dios Creador te ama.

Basado en el texto original escrito por Michael Ketterhagen. Un agradecimiento especial a los padres Paul Niemann y Joe Kempf. Editado por Marco Batta. Diseño de Maggie Bubenik.

Publicado con aprobación eclesiástica. Textos tomados del Ritual para la Confirmación, Editorial Buena Prensa 1999. Impreso en Estados Unidos.

LIBROS LIGUORI

ISBN 978-0-7648-2378-7

9 780764 823787 50000>

Based on the original by Michael Ketterhagen. Special thanks to Rev. Paul Niemann and Rev. Joe Kempf.

Edited by Lauren K. Borstell.

Design by Maggie Bubenik.

Published with ecclesiastical approval. Compliant with *The Roman Missal*, third edition. Printed in U.S.A.